The Book of
KINGSKERSWELL

The Parish and its People

CARSEWELLA LOCAL HISTORY GROUP

HALSGROVE

First published in Great Britain in 2003.

Copyright © 2003 Carsewella Local History Group.

*All rights reserved. No part of this publication may be reproduced,
stored in a retrieval system, or transmitted in any form or by any
means without the prior permission of the copyright holder.*

British Library Cataloguing-in-Publication Data.
A CIP record for this title is available from the British Library.

ISBN 1 84114 236 0

HALSGROVE

Halsgrove House
Lower Moor Way
Tiverton, Devon EX16 6SS
Tel: 01884 243242
Fax: 01884 243325
email: sales@halsgrove.com
website: www.halsgrove.com

Frontispiece photograph: *Afternoon tea in the garden of Holmleigh, Fluder Hill, July 1923.*
Left to right: *Mary Ravenscroft, mother pouring tea, Sybil Laura Ravenscroft.*

Printed and bound by CPI Bath Press, Bath.

*Whilst every care has been taken to ensure the accuracy of the
information contained in this book, the publisher disclaims responsibility
for any mistakes which may have been inadvertently included.*

Foreword

This book is the culmination of the first eight years of Carsewella, the Kingskerswell Local History Group. It is presented as a fitting tribute to the daily life and work, personal reminiscences and experiences, and social activities of the people of Kingskerswell, and also includes something of its history and early origins. We are indebted to many, both in the parish and beyond, for the wealth of personal stories, anecdotes and personal photographs which, when added to the archive material already held, amount to far more than can possibly be included in this book. The most difficult decisions have been principally concerned with not so much as what to retain, as what to defer for later use. Many contributors have not been named directly, the community aspect being considered more relevant.

Special thanks are due to Gerald Quinn, who not only edited but also compiled much of this volume. He could not have possibly achieved this work without the valuable and eagle-eyed assistance of the editorial steering group. Their patience, as also Naomi's at Halsgrove, is greatly appreciated.

The publishers have performed wonders with the texts and pictorial elements, and Halsgrove have produced a lovely and attractive archive of a book which we in Carsewella feel sure will become more than just a coffee-table decoration, if not indeed preferred reading on life in Kingskerswell.

It is sincerely hoped that the gremlins have been well and truly banished. For any errors or unintended omissions the editor offers, on behalf of Carsewella and himself, his most profound apologies.

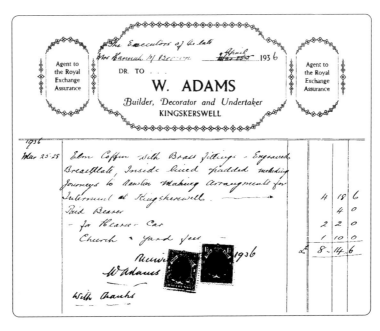

Receipted invoice of W. Adams.

God's Acres

Bird's-eye view of God's Acres.

God's Acres

English Dust is English Soil

Indian Imperial Police (retired)
Kenmore
College Road
Dec. 3rd 1935

Sir,

Under the wise guidance of the Great Creator, Englishmen, women and children have carried the clay of which they are formed to distant lands for their enrichment. Here in Devon, they lie side by side tended by loving hands. In the desert and the jungle their dust is at the mercy of the four winds; but it is always England's messenger on virgin soil.

A short while ago chance led my footsteps along the road which passes the Kingskerswell Parish Church. As I halted beside the murmuring stream hastening on its way to the sea, and gazed across it and a low moss-covered stone wall, I saw before me God's own garden.

In the foreground were graves, on a green velvet lawn, laid in symmetrical order, covered with fresh and lovely flowers placed by loving hands in memory of the dead.

In the background a hill, gently sloping, beautified by trees with leaves of many colours, all blended with the sky and their surroundings.

On my right were the Church and an arched gateway, both with time's hand resting on them. Within the entrance gateway were rough-hewn slabs of stone for whosoever wished to rest upon them.

On my left was an apple orchard, behind which could be seen old-fashioned thatched cottages and a farmhouse.

As I stood in contemplation, my attention was attracted by the figure of a villager dressed in blue overalls, resting in the gateway. I joined him and mentioned how the scene had impressed and affected me.

I said: 'You people of Kingskerswell are indeed worthy children of the Great Gardener and Artist. I have never seen a more beautiful sight or better kept 'God's Acre' in my life and I have travelled much.'

He replied, like a flash: 'We do not take any credit to ourselves. The picture you admire was easy for us to make when the Almighty gave us such a wonderful frame to set it in.'

The man who said this to me was a workman earning thirty-five shillings a week, and reminded me of the 'Village blacksmith beneath the spreading chestnut tree, with large and sinewy hands.' An Englishman! It made me say to myself: 'Tell him to go to the top of the table' and I did. I took my proper place at the bottom, but hope some day to sit beside him: the man in blue overalls.

Yours truly,
R.P. LAMBERT

(A letter to the Editor, *Newton Abbot & Mid-Devon Times*)

Fore Street looking towards Fluder Hill.

Contents

	Foreword	3
	Letter to the Editor, Newton Abbot & Mid-Devon Times	5
	Acknowledgements	9
Chapter 1:	AROUND THE VILLAGE & PARISH	15
Chapter 2:	PLACES OF WORSHIP	41
Chapter 3:	MANORS	51
Chapter 4:	THE RAILWAY	55
Chapter 5:	THE PARISH COMES OF AGE	61
Chapter 6:	VILLAGE LIFE RECALLED	67
Chapter 7:	WHEN WE WERE SO VERY YOUNG	87
Chapter 8:	ASPECTS OF FARMING	93
Chapter 9:	THE WAR YEARS	103
Chapter 10:	PARISH EVENTS & PASTIMES	115
Chapter 11:	PERSONALITIES: A MISCELLANY	145
Chapter 12:	BARTON HALL	153
	Subscribers	157

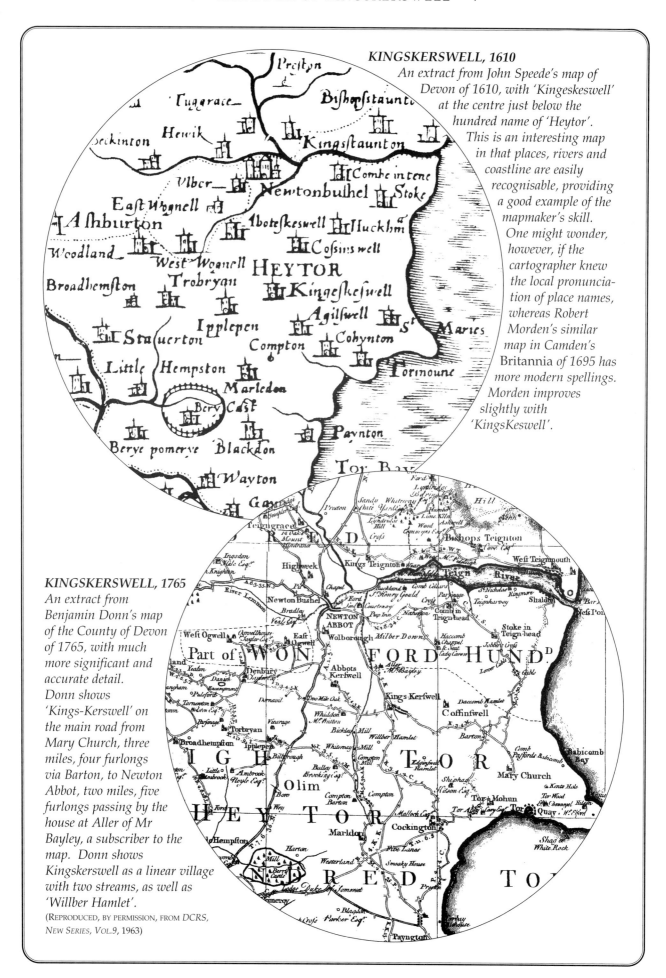

KINGSKERSWELL, 1610
An extract from John Speede's map of Devon of 1610, with 'Kingeskeswell' at the centre just below the hundred name of 'Heytor'. This is an interesting map in that places, rivers and coastline are easily recognisable, providing a good example of the mapmaker's skill. One might wonder, however, if the cartographer knew the local pronunciation of place names, whereas Robert Morden's similar map in Camden's Britannia of 1695 has more modern spellings. Morden improves slightly with 'KingsKeswell'.

KINGSKERSWELL, 1765
An extract from Benjamin Donn's map of the County of Devon of 1765, with much more significant and accurate detail. Donn shows 'Kings-Kerswell' on the main road from Mary Church, three miles, four furlongs via Barton, to Newton Abbot, two miles, five furlongs passing by the house at Aller of Mr Bayley, a subscriber to the map. Donn shows Kingskerswell as a linear village with two streams, as well as 'Willber Hamlet'.
(REPRODUCED, BY PERMISSION, FROM DCRS, NEW SERIES, VOL.9, 1963)

Acknowledgements

The editor wishes to place on record his personal thanks to members of his long-suffering family, friends (has he any left?), and all those lovely people, not forgetting their canine friends and moggies, in and around the village and parish of Kingskerswell for their precious trust and forbearance. Oh, and in case he forgets, to members of Carsewella for their spontaneous response to Naomi's initial approach regarding this project, his heartfelt response, viz. 'Go raibh maith agat'. Carsewella gratefully acknowledges the generous support received from Kingskerswell Parish Council during this project.

Carsewella acknowledges, with grateful thanks, the sympathetic and inestimable help and assistance from staff at Kingskerswell, Newton Abbot, Exeter, and Torquay Libraries, and all those people (not forgetting our absent friends – RIP) who have contributed articles, stories, photographs, etc. They are: Annie Marsh Adams, John Andrews, David Beer, Stan Blackmore, Lea Bond, Boo, Janet Bowers, Dennis Bramble, Fred Brimecombe, Topline Broadhurst, Mr and Mrs T.H.L. Brown, John and Sandra Cann, Janet Carter, Mrs Chappell, Les Cheesman, Norman Cooper, Norah Cornish, Mr and Mrs Syd Crocker, Alan and Sylvia Davies, Eileen Davies, Mr and Mrs Fred Dodd, Carol Durston, Annette Everett, Winifred Farley, Dorothy Fogwill, Mrs Force, Sid Gale (RIP), W.M. Gane, Joy Garner, Peter Gray, David Grylls, John and Pat Hartley, Robert and Winifred Hern, Sheila Jeffery, Margaret Jury, Marilyn Kenyon, Janet King, Maggie King, Mrs Langabeer, Revd John Leonard, Rod and Louise Lewis, Grahame and Susan Luscombe, Norah Luxton, Margaret Matthews, Mike and Lynn McElheron, Charlotte Mertens, Frank, Loveday and Rachel Middlebrook, Richard Miller, Bert Mitchell, Charlie Moon, Mr and Mrs Mudge, George Mulkern, Ken Nayler (RIP), Mr A.J. (Tony) Pain, Gerry and Gwen Palmer, Richard Peters, Maurice Petherick, John Pike, Douglas, Judy, Matthew and Fionnuala Quinn, Graham and Gill Rawle, Rosko (RIP), Vi Rowe, Alan Salsbury, Sasha, Constance Scotter-Owen, Shan, Sophie, Harry Stephens, Jack Terrell, John and Eileen Tibbetts, Paul Venn Dunn, Rhoda Wakeham, Jane Wale, Lesley Watson, Joy Welch, Michael Wells, Vic Willis (RIP), George Wills.

Official permissions were sought, and gratefully obtained, from: Ordnance Survey, Romsey Road, Southampton, as noted on the map extracts; *Herald Express* Publications, Torquay, for use of photographs; *Torquay Times* and Tindle Newspapers Limited, for use of photographs; David & Charles Limited, for the early Ordnance Survey (1809) map extract; The Olde Map Co., Sennen Cove, Penzance, for the extract from John Speede's 1610 map; Dr Todd Gray, for use of material from 'Early Stuart Mariners and Shipping' (*DCRS Vol.33*); Mary Ravenhill and Devon and Cornwall Record Society, for the extract from 'Benjamin Donn, A Map of the County of Devon 1765' (*DCRS Vol.9*).

The editor formally acknowledges the singular and valued help, and in particular the patience, of the 'editorial group', namely Annette Everett, Dennis Bramble, Mike McElheron and Frank Middlebrook.

Please accept apologies on behalf of 'Carsewella' for inadvertent misrepresentations, errors and omissions. Every effort has been made to eliminate these where possible. For any which have slipped our notice the editor bears full responsibility. (He has the sneaking suspicion that that's why he got the job.)

CARSEWELLA (KINGSKERSWELL LOCAL HISTORY GROUP)

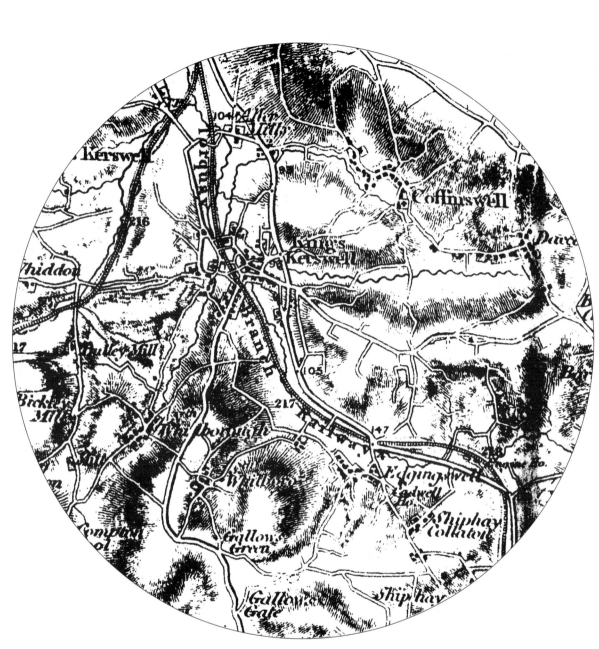

KINGSKERSWELL, 1809
An extract from the first edition of the Ordnance Survey of 1809, with railways included to 1883. This map now has hachures for indicating hills, etc., and many more roads, lanes and streams are named; a greater number of place names and spot heights are given, and, for the railways, distances from London are included. Kingskerswell now has six streams marked, the unique boundary wall of Kerswell Down is given and Whilborough Common is outlined (although neither is named). The village road pattern is now more evident as is the Yon Street development. The railway cuts dramatically through the village, showing a disregard for community unity and harmony.

(REPRODUCED, BY PERMISSION, FROM THE 1809 ORDNANCE SURVEY MAP)

MAPS

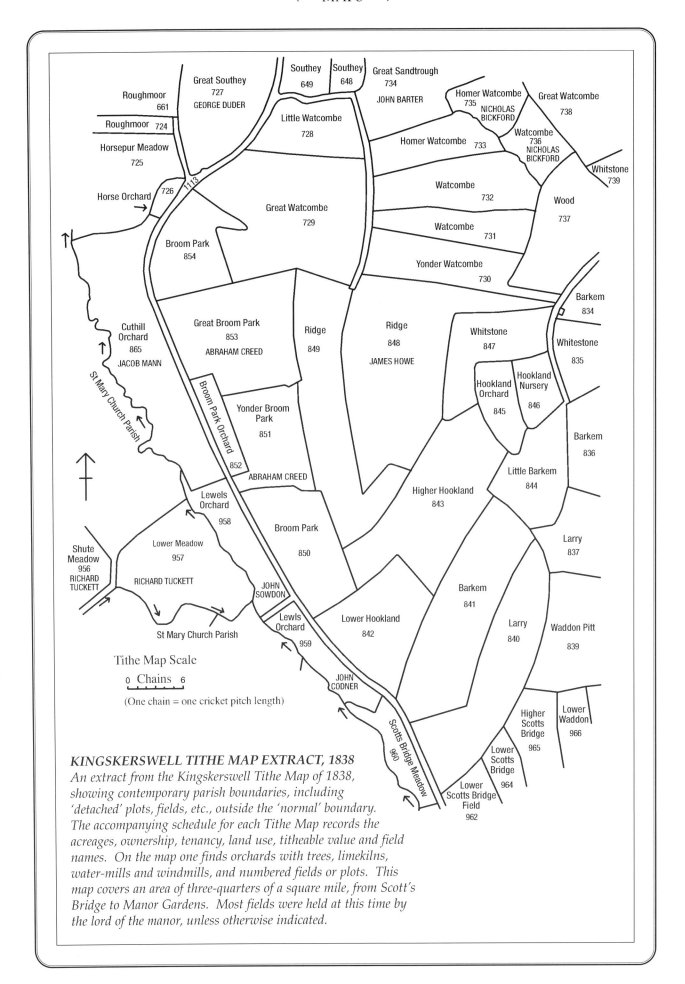

KINGSKERSWELL TITHE MAP EXTRACT, 1838
An extract from the Kingskerswell Tithe Map of 1838, showing contemporary parish boundaries, including 'detached' plots, fields, etc., outside the 'normal' boundary. The accompanying schedule for each Tithe Map records the acreages, ownership, tenancy, land use, titheable value and field names. On the map one finds orchards with trees, limekilns, water-mills and windmills, and numbered fields or plots. This map covers an area of three-quarters of a square mile, from Scott's Bridge to Manor Gardens. Most fields were held at this time by the lord of the manor, unless otherwise indicated.

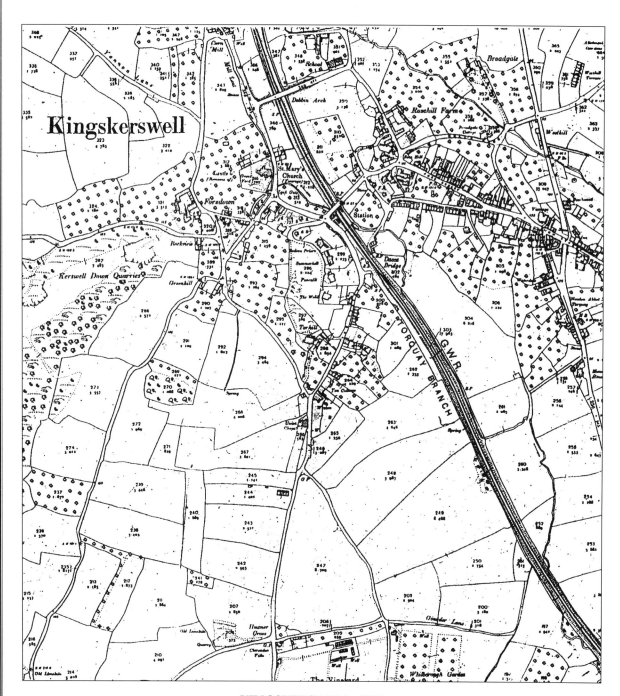

KINGSKERSWELL, 1905
Orchards at one time were an important element in the local economy, Kingskerswell being widely known for its cider production. This extract from the Ordnance Survey map published in 1905 shows a very clear difference in the character of the village landscape as it appeared then, when compared with the consolidated built-up residential development of a century later. Practically all of the cider orchards east of the railway and several on The Tors and in the Yon Street area have since given way to housing.

(REPRODUCED, BY PERMISSION, FROM THE 1905 ORDNANCE SURVEY MAP)

MAPS

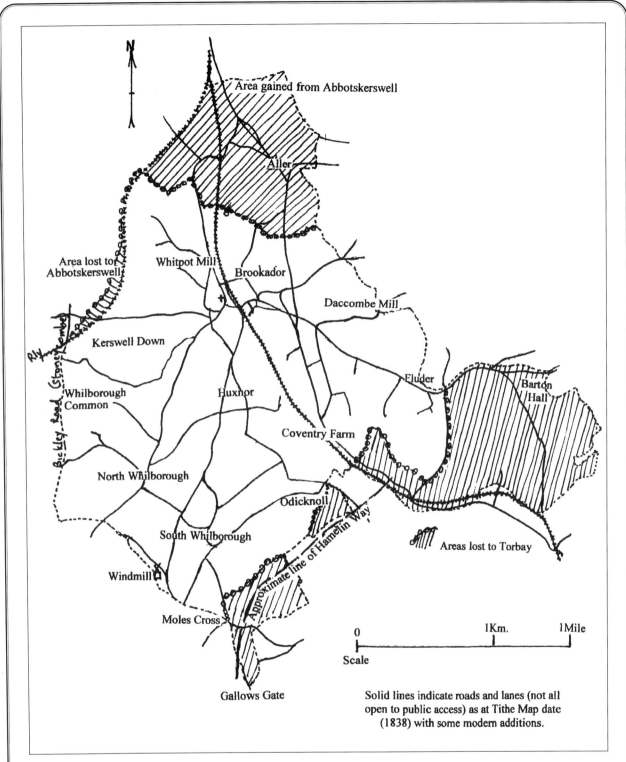

**PARISH OF KINGSKERSWELL
WITH MINOR MODIFICATIONS FROM THE 1997 ORDNANCE SURVEY MAP**

This map shows the Tithe Map parish boundary, and alterations since 1838 resulting from official boundary revisions (excluding detached areas, within and without the continuous boundary). Shown are areas lost to Torbay and Abbotskerswell, and areas gained from Abbotskerswell. Also shown are: Aller, Whitpot Mill, Brookador, Daccombe Mill, Kerswell Down, Whilborough Common, Huxnor, Fluder, Barton Hall, Coventry Farm, North Whilborough, South Whilborough, Odicknoll, Windmill, Moles Cross and Gallows Gate, and the approximate line of Hamelin Way. (REPRODUCED, BY PERMISSION, FROM THE 1997 ORDNANCE SURVEY MAP)

Right: *Torquay Road and Fluder Hill.*

Looking across Southey Lane to Fluder Hill.

This picture and right: *Windmill ruins, Moles Lane, in 1997, since converted into a holiday home.*

Chapter 1

AROUND THE VILLAGE & PARISH

AN INTERVIEW WITH BILL BOVEY

Mr Kenneth C. Nayler interviewed Bill Bovey on four separate occasions, twice in August 1996, and again in both February and April 1997. At our Carsewella Local History Group meetings, Ken would ask us for questions to put to Bill on his visits, sure in the gleeful knowledge of the strawberry and cream treat awaiting him on his arrival. Sadly both gentlemen have since passed away. Naturally, topics were approached as they presented themselves and many were returned to on several occasions. What follows represents the consolidated fruits and gems of their chats on these occasions, presented with few but minor modifications.

I had the pleasure of interviewing Mr William Bovey at his home on Dartmoor. 'Bill Bovey', as he likes to be called, lives with his daughter, Brenda, in a very old but interesting cottage, built of granite, miles from anywhere. The deeds show that the property dates back to 1260. Bill was born in Kingskerswell and kept the Old Bakery until he left the village in 1947.

No.25 Fore Street

He lived in a property known as 'Kismet', No.25 Fore Street, which is roughly where the Co-op and car park are now. Fronting Fore Street, No.25 occupied the whole of the space taken up by the Co-op and car park. His own cottage was next to No.27, that is, next to the Co-op. The property abutted the pavement and its

A view from Yannon Lane.

Sedgewell Lane.

Above: *Tor Hill Cottage, Greenhill Road, 1905.*

Left: *Tor Hill House, Greenhill Road, 2003.*

Right: *The cottage which stood at the junction of Greenhill Road and Churchway Lane.*

Left: *A modern view of the dwelling at the junction of Greenhill Road and Churchway Lane.*

frontage was in the form of a small shop which his wife looked after between the wars; she sold sweets. Beside the shop on the Pharmacy side (the Pharmacy is No.23) was a reasonably high wall enclosing a high garden and behind his property he had 2½ acres of ground.

'Ye Olde Bakery'

Bill looked after 'Ye Olde Bakery'. [Rose Hill Close occupies this site at the time of going to press.] The Bakery had been built in 1890 by a Mr Crocker and when completed it was 'let' to Bill Bovey's father. Bill took it on at his father's death and operated it until he left the village in 1947, so it was in the family for 57 years. Apparently a large proportion of the property at the turn of the century belonged to Mr Crocker, who was described as a very good landlord. Bill says he is no relation to Sydney Crocker still living in the village.

Fore Street Shops

The Post Office was built in the 1890s along with most of the other properties on that side of the street. It was operated as a butcher's shop, at first by the Crockers but later on it passed to the Ball family. Fred Ball's mother was one of Dickie French's family, another family of butchers. Bill believed that the first people to operate the shop now known as 'Manor Pharmacy' were some people called Skinner. They had it for many years as a hardware and oil store. Later on it passed to a family named Taylor and they were there for a year or two before it passed to the Sagars. It was a fantastic shop and they sold everything you could think of in the ironmongery and hardware line, including paraffin oil. Mrs Sagar retired from there when the Manor Pharmacy moved there from the main road in the 1970s. In the early 1980s, a lady dentist opened a practice up over the shop; there had never been a dentist in the village before. She eventually passed the practice over to Mr Neil Black.

The Condition of Fore Street

Bill described the road surface as being very rough and rutted, but no one took much notice of that because he said that it had not been so very long before he was born that Fore Street was a 'dirt road'; he explained that his father and grandfather knew the road only as hard-packed in summer and a sea of mud in winter, with occasional harder areas where people had placed the ashes from their fire grates, or buckets of stones from their gardens in the road in an attempt to 'firm' it up a little bit. But in the 1890s 'they', presumably the Local Government Board, had quarry stone chippings put on the road and rolled in. The road surface area was not made into a tarmacadam road until after the First World War in 1919.

Old Names for Fore Street

I asked if he knew anything about the old names for Fore Street, being at one time Main Street up to the top of the

Ye Olde Bakery, Fore Street (now Rose Hill Close).

Rock View, Kings Hill, c.1910.

A.M. Davey's store (now Beggar's Banquet), Fore Street.

The Tors.

The Tors from Daccabridge Road.

Kingskerswell from Tor Hill (The Tors).

The Motor Cycle Action Group protesting against compulsory wearing of crash helmets, viewed from Kingskerswell Arch, mid-1970s.

AROUND THE VILLAGE & PARISH

Arch and Regent Street from the Arch to Fluder Hill. He said he had no knowledge of this and had never heard his father or grandfather mention it.

Street Lights
Bill described the street lights as square wooden posts set for the most part in the carriageway, not the pavement. On top of the posts were oil-lamps looked after by a man called Prosser.

Traffic
In his young days Bill said there was very little traffic in the village. There were more cows driven through the street than there was traffic and the cows used to leave behind a succession of 'pats' along the street and pavement so when walking you had to be careful where you stepped. It was particularly mucky walking about on dark winter evenings; every house and shop had boot scrapers and boot brushes outside their premises. There was quite a bit of horse-drawn traffic – carts, wains, drays, etc., together with gigs, carriages, phaetons, traps, etc. The first car in the village belonged to Dr Hatfield who lived and operated his surgery on The Tors. Bill believed the first car operated by Dr Hatfield was a Ford and he employed a driver named Billy Holmes. Apparently Billy Holmes did quite well for himself because he married the doctor's housekeeper and they had two children.

Village Doctors
Doctor Hatfield took over the practice in 1906. It had previously been run from the same place by a Doctor MacDonald who had the practice in 1890. Bill did not know if there was a doctor here before that. Dr Hatfield had a son, Teddy, who followed a career in the Army. His daughter married a man named Sawyer and emigrated to South America and they in turn had a son. The doctor's wife, a well-known figure and very pleasant, had a horse called 'Dobbin' on which she went all around the district and after which she named the railway arch and road.

Dr MacDonald travelled on his rounds in a phaeton, a four-wheeled light carriage with or without a top.

I asked him about Doctor George Francis Symons, who, records show, had been a doctor in Kingskerswell. He replied that he only knew about Doctor MacDonald from what his father had told him. I have it on good authority that Doctor Symons operated a practice here until about 1889 but I don't know when he started. The beautiful brass lectern in the Parish Church was presented by 'Many friends of George Francis Symons a worshipper at the church, who had been the village doctor in Kingskerswell.' The lectern was first used at Easter 1889. A brass plate on the pillar by the organ records this fact.

Roads Again
Returning to the roads – Bill Bovey said that the other roads in and around the village were in the same state or even worse than Fore Street when he was a small lad. Of the main road (now the A380) he said that quarry stone was put on that as a dressing probably about ten years before the minor roads and village main street, so his father had told him. His grandfather had told him that Fore Street, Kingskerswell, only came into prominence after Brunel built the railway line through the village in the 1840s – the line had opened for trains in 1849. Though the street existed, there were few buildings on it beyond its junction with Daccabridge Road. As he previously said, most of the buildings, mainly on the Bakery side, were owned by Mr Crocker.

Daccabridge Road
Daccabridge Road was the main street through to Yon Street and there was one shop in it that he can remember and that was roughly opposite the slip-road that goes up to Fore Street opposite what is now the car park. Bill remembers it as a general shop that sold all manner of goods, not food as he recalls. When the shop eventually closed and was converted to a dwelling-house, one of Billy Adams' workmen was pushing a wheelbarrow through the front door and, just inside, the floor collapsed under the weight of the barrow and its contents. It appears that there was a well there, one of the 18 wells in the village. Apparently it had been boarded over and someone, he knows not whom, stated that they remembered the well from years ago. The wheelbarrow disappeared from sight...

Bill said his old grandfather remembered there being a well which was fairly constantly used, directly in the line of the railway and Kingskerswell Station when they were built in the 1840s. The old South Devon Railway Company, which subsequently became the GWR, covered the well but piped the water supply to a large wall-mounted cast-iron pump affixed to the wall in the entrance to the old Daccabridge Road-Yon Street junction. I am reliably informed by Mr and Mrs Hern of Daccabridge Road that some of the old pump remains are still there but covered in weeds. The wall is thickly overgrown with ivy and brambles. [This area is on private ground.] Daccabridge Road in Bill's young days was always known as 'Underway'.

Daccabridge Road from The Tors.

Billy Adams' coffin workshop, Daccabridge Road.

Codner's cider barn, Daccabridge Road.

The barn which once stood on Daccabridge orchard.

More Wells
Continuing on the subject of wells, one that is fairly evident still is in Water Lane opposite the top of Sunnyside where there is a small arch in the wall below the main A380 road. Bill also mentioned one in Yon Street but not exactly where – it was not where the old pump used to be on the wall of the old junction of Daccabridge and Yon Street. He mentioned that there is a well under the centre of the village car park, because that used to be his garden when he lived at 'Kismet' in Fore Street. He also mentioned a well outside the front door of No.26 Fore Street, which is where the old fruit and grocer's shop kept by his uncle Charles Hodge-Brooks used to be.

More Shops
Bill's old grandfather told him that several shops existed around the junction of Fore Street and Water Lane. The shop on the corner of Water Lane which has just closed and been converted into a dwelling was at one time the Co-op. The present Co-op was built and operated from 1946 when [it] moved from the corner of Water Lane, but it was a bit smaller then as it has been extended since. The car park was built in the early 1970s. From the old Co-op, immediately around the corner next door in Fore Street, was another shop, now a dwelling. One can still see marks of the conversion over the front living-room window. This was Brimson's shop. He sold boots and shoes and did repairs to footwear too. It is one of Brimson's relatives who has the barber's shop by Devon Square in Newton Abbot. Bill said that he had told him Brimson 'put in' for the public hangman's job years ago but he was beaten to the job by Pierpoint who since kept a public house in Lancashire. There was a butcher's shop on the other corner of Water Lane with a slaughterhouse behind it in Water Lane. This shop fronted Fore Street. In Bill Bovey's young days it was kept by a chap called Dickie French.

I told Bill I had seen a photograph of a young lad standing in the middle of the road by Water Lane [see p21], who I believed was called Osborne. Bill said he was one of a family who lived over in Yon Street. That particular lad was a soldier in the First World War. [George Arthur Osborne, Cpl, RMLI – see Grave No.1/13/659 in the Village War Memorial list.] He had two sisters, one named Jane. One of them retired to South Africa.

A Lucky Escape
The first shop on the main A380 occupied as a newsagent's was MacDonald's where 'Kerswell News' is now. The only thing Bill could recall about them was that in the 1940s their daughter nearly blew herself and the premises up when she was playing with the fireworks stored in the shop. In Water Lane on the right-hand side going up the hill there were no buildings, only a V-shaped garden there opposite No.10 Water Lane. Next door to French's butcher's shop going towards Fluder Hill was the public house known formerly as Trott's Hotel because it was kept by a man called Trott.

Trott's Hotel
The next tenant of Trott's Hotel was Tommy Burns. Bill believed that by this time it was known as the Seven Stars, probably after the Parish Church. [The parish stocks have seven holes and St Mary's crown traditionally has seven stars.] The next tenant was Bill Bovey's uncle, Bill Milton, who took it over just before the First World War. The last landlord of the Seven Stars before it was demolished in 1963 was a Mr Bert Low. The last butcher on the corner next to the Seven Stars was Oliver French, whose father was Dickie French. Apparently Oliver used to visit the Seven Stars quite frequently during the day, between customers, just to have a quick nip of whisky.

AROUND THE VILLAGE & PARISH

Fore Street from the junction of Water Lane, looking towards Fluder Hill.

Left: *Fore Street from the junction of Water Lane, looking towards Fluder Hill. French's Butchers and the Seven Stars Hotel are on the right and Moores Bakery is on the left.*

Trott's Seven Stars Hotel, Fore Street.

21

Brewery

There was a brewery roughly on the junction of what is now Marguerite Way. It was built by William Mortimer and brewed beer only. William Mortimer also owned eight or ten public houses of which The Park Inn was one. They were only beerhouses – no wines, spirits, etc. The brewery was closed between the First and Second World Wars, when old William Mortimer died. Bill Bovey stressed the fact that Billy Mortimer was an extremely pleasant man and good to the local people. He was on the Board of Governors at the hospital.

Yon Street

Another shop he mentioned, now closed and adjacent to the postbox set in the wall, was in Yon Street. In his young days it was kept by a Miss Hill and sold general goods and groceries on a small scale. Bill said he never remembered it being a Post Office in spite of the adjacent postbox but they did sell stamps. After Miss Hill the shop was taken over by Jack Brooks who retired in 1945 when he sold the business to the Martins. Jack Brooks ran a taxi in the village until 1950. Yon Street store was still in existence in 1982.

Brookador

Mr Milverton kept a slaughterhouse in Brookador and sold meat around the village from a horse-drawn vehicle. Bill could not recall any other shops in Yon Street, School Road, Church End Road or Brookador.

Daccabridge Road and St Mary's Road

I brought Bill back to the subject of roads and asked if his grandfather or uncles had ever mentioned Daccabridge Road and St Mary's before the railway was built. His grandfather had said that Daccabridge Road definitely went across and formed quite a wide junction with Yon Street. The evidence is still there. The road was cut by the railway and had been too low down to form a bridge over the railway or to form a pass under the railway because of flooding.

Of St Mary's he said that his grandfather was sure that the road from the bend in Pound Lane went right down across what is now the railway line and came out in front of Brook Cottage opposite the Parish Church's north lych-gate.

Railway Gangers

I asked if he remembered who worked on the Railway in his young days. I mentioned the names of Gang Inspector G. Reynolds and Ganger Perryman. Bill said he did not know of them but recalled Gangers Mead and Burn when he was very young. Ganger Burn's daughter kept the shop on the corner of Water Lane which she later sold to the Co-op between the wars.

Water Rights

Bill mentioned water rights; he stated that in the old days of working mills, of which Whitpot was one, the rights to the water in streams was extremely important. Mill owners would buy out water rights to a stream and any leat would be owned absolutely by the miller as the leat had to be built at considerable expense. The water rights in the stream coming down from Scott's Bridge were solely owned by the millers of Whitpot and Decoy Mills. Decoy Mill was situated to the rear of the Keyberry Inn and it closed as a grist-mill about 12–18 months after Whitpot. In Bill's young days and up to the 1920s the miller at Whitpot was a Mr Floyd.

Church Street (now Church End Road), c.1922. The thatched barn was destroyed by Frank White's steam lorry in the early 1920s.

AROUND THE VILLAGE & PARISH

Floyd's Mill, 1914.

Brass Band
There had been a very efficient brass band in Kingskerswell, which played at many functions in the village and surrounding areas right up to the beginning of the First World War, but it was discontinued then because many of the players went into the Army. Bill believed that the instruments probably finished up with the military also.

Dog Track
On the subject of the dog track, Bill stated that it was probably opened in the 1930s and ran for about 30 years to the early 1960s, being operated by people called Bright. Dog racing was very popular and had a large following. The track was in the three-acre field now known as Stadium Drive. [On the 1840 Tithe Map this field, of area three acres, one rood and three perches, was called Horsespur Meadow.] There were properly constructed dog kennels running at right angles to the road, a small covered stadium and refreshment area all heated by overhead gas heaters. The Tote operated from one end of the stadium with a covered area for several bookmakers. The pedestrian entrance had a gate with turnstile through the high hedge opposite the old 'Halfway House Inn' which still stands near the junction of Southey Lane with the main A380. The old public house was closed when the Hare and Hounds was built in the 1960s. The old inn may have been one of those owned by Billy Mortimer but Bill was not sure.

The fields that are now known as Stadium Drive and Roundmoors were originally owned by Devonshire Dairies. Prior to being owned by the Bright brothers, these two fields, together with others alongside, were always known as the Pony Fields. Pony racing was held over a total of three fields, including what became the racetrack, on several occasions each year. Bill's father used to hire a marquee and pitch it beside the course and do the catering both for the pony racing and the fêtes that used to be held on the fields.

Football Clubs
Bill stated that the Aller Vale Football Club and Rugby Club used to play on those fields up to the First World

A view from the fields at the bottom of Southey Lane with the old Halfway House Inn on the left.

A view of Kingskerswell from the Downs.

23

The village from the Downs.

The Squire's Quarry, Maddacombe Road, c.1905.

War. Between the wars the Football Club used to play up on the Downs. The pitch ran from the broken rail overlooking Maddacombe Quarry to the woods running down the slope, in other words at right angles to the pathway as one walks across the Downs. Cricket was also played on the Downs with the head of the pitch on one side of the football pitch; the pitch ran parallel with the pathway.

Fêtes
The fêtes ceased just prior to the First World War. They tried to restart them again in the early 1920s but they were not a success so they were discontinued completely until restarted on the Church Meadow under the auspices of the church in 1990.

Brooklea Tea Gardens
I asked about 'Brooklea Tea Gardens'. Bill said that these were the site of what became the new Seven Stars in 1963/4 (now the 'Sloop'). There was a ten-foot-high brick wall alongside the main A380 road, and up at the top of the site, probably where the back pub 'car park' is now, was a bungalow, built by a Newton Abbot builder (name unknown) for his retirement. Bill did not know how long he lived there. The Brooklea Tea Garden was certainly on the site of the 'Sloop', but it only occupied a small portion of it.

The Princess Road council-houses behind the 'Sloop' were all built in the 1920s by Tom Woollacott and Billy Adams.

Blacksmiths
I asked Bill about blacksmiths. He said that there were three. One was in School Road adjacent to the junction of Pound Lane, where the doors are now painted pale blue. There was another forge [associated with this business] nearby, and both were always busy in Bill's young days, and operated by a smallish man named Silas Hill, and his son. Silas had a full set of whiskers. As an aside, Bill said that when the parish bounds were beaten in the early 1920s, it was found that previously the complete boundary was never covered, as somewhere near Kerswell Gardens that is now, the road went over a long culvert and the culvert was never traversed. As Silas Hill was a very small chap he volunteered to crawl through the culvert, and he did. Silas was a general blacksmith and always busy. There was a milkman named Gordon Hill who was Silas's grandson. Gordon's father Fred Hill worked in the railway workshops in Newton Abbot.

Bob Jury operated a forge and wheelwrighting business at Jury's Corner. He had a chap we knew as Diffy Dillon working for him. Diffy was stone deaf but a good workman and apparently it was Diffy who built the forge, etc. for Bob. Most of their work was coachbuilding and carts and carriages and wheelwrighting. Bob Jury's forge closed in 1948. He made traps and light wagons right up until the First World War.

The other blacksmith was Mr Neck in Fore Street behind what is now 'Forge Cottage', near the Co-op. There is a narrow drangway between Forge Cottage and No.27 next door. Some few years ago there were timbers running between the two cottages with a corrugated-iron covering so that it made a dry passageway in rainy weather. Apparently most of Mr Neck's trade was shoeing horses as the drangway was only wide enough for a horse and not for large equipment.

Hunt Meeting
I was told that the hunt used to 'meet' occasionally outside Silas Hill's smithy. Bill stated that they were advertised as meeting outside Mr Foss' farm opposite the smithy, but no doubt Silas Hill used to pick up some shoeing business from the hunt.

Charlie Foss was the father of Peter Foss who was the last tenant of the farm before it was sold by the squire (who was the owner) to the Health Authority for the building of the present Health Centre. Old Charlie emigrated to Canada, but Bill did not know when.

Farmer Hodge
I enquired about Farmer Hodge and when he lived. He was referred to as a farmer, but he was really a smallholder. He had two cows which he kept on the field that is now Church Meadow, where the church car park is now; this was before the First World War. He lived in one of the cottages in Fore Street opposite the present Co-op.

St Mary's Garage
Bill stated that St Mary's Garage in Fore Street was

AROUND THE VILLAGE & PARISH

Right: *Fore Street/Water Lane junction, 2003.*

Main Street (Fore Street), c.1932.

built by Vic Baldwin, with the aid of a loan from Bill, and Vic operated the garage for several years up to the late 1960s–early 1970s. Previously there was an orchard on the site.

Tennis Courts
Apparently there was a court at Broadgate owned by a Captain Stokes who sold it to a Mr Lancaster but Bill does not know when it was closed. There was another court behind Billy Mortimer's brewery, but he didn't know when that closed either. There is also the court up on The Tors; the remains are still there and badly overgrown. Bill stated that this court was owned by Dr Hatfield and was laid down by him, and looked after by Billy Holmes.

The A380 Road
Bill informed me that his grandfather, and indeed his great-grandfather whom he had known as a young boy, had told him that prior to the building of the railway in the 1840s, the road we now know as the A380 did not exist. The main road had been built at about the same time as the railway was opened in about 1848/49, but it was only a minor road or lane in those days. The widest part of the whole road was the archway at Kingskerswell, which had been built by partially tunnelling and excavating under the escarpment formed by Fluder Hill and Fore Street.

The Lord Nelson
Bill's grandfather did not think that the Lord Nelson was there at that time but that all the cottages on the higher side of the inn were, and they seemed old in [his] granddad's time.

Pinsents, brewers of Newton Abbot, had the Lord Nelson Inn before it was taken over by Symonds the brewers. Apparently George Facey, for a long time a bell-ringer and sidesman at the church, was related to the Pinsents.

The British Legion Club used to hold their meetings in the large room behind the Lord Nelson Inn but the club closed soon after the Second World War. Their 'standard' still hangs in the church.

The Easterbrooks
There were really no houses on what was the A380 in his young days but around 1910 Mr Easterbrook, a farmer who came from Tavistock, had 'Trevenn House' built. He had two sons, the eldest was Dick and the second was Tom who went to school with Bill. Tom was very brainy and eventually qualified as a solicitor and had a practice in Torquay. Old Tom kept the practice going and Bill believed his son went into it. There was also a daughter who lived in Trevenn House right up to the Second World War, and she was on her own there for several years after the old man died. She was still there in 1948. The field in which Trevenn House was built belonged to John Banbury. After the construction of Trevenn House, Southey Drive was added.

The Manor House on the A380
Bill said that the building known as the 'Manor House' on the A380 was originally built at the same time as the old main road was built in the 1840s. The so-called

Broadgate

Right: *Broadgate Lodge, 1907.*

Left: *Broadgate Lodge, c.1920*

Below: *The Avenue, Broadgate.*

Broadgate, where Broadgate Road now stands.

AROUND THE VILLAGE & PARISH

Kingskerswell Arch

Left: *The north side of Kingskerswell Arch before road widening in 1963.*

Right: *Kingskerswell Arch roadworks in front of the Public Hall.*

Above: *Kingskerswell Arch, southern approach, early-twentieth century. Also in view is the thatched cottage opposite Mortimore's General Stores.*

Right: *Kingskerswell Arch, southern approach, 1957.*

Kingskerswell Arch

Kingskerswell Arch, southern approach, during road widening

Left: *The south side of Kingskerswell Arch during alterations.*

Right: *The south side of Kingskerswell Arch during alterations.*

Left: *The south side of Kingskerswell Arch after alterations.*

AROUND THE VILLAGE & PARISH

'Manor House' was used as a coaching house and was altered over the years before it was eventually demolished a few years ago, and a modern block of flats erected in its place.

Coventry Farm

I asked Bill the original use of Coventry Farm House. It belonged to Devonshire Dairies, and butter and cream were despatched from there to the London area markets. Sam Lake was the manager and lived at the farmhouse. All the land on the right-hand side of the road going towards Torquay belonged to the dairy company. The farm dates back to the time before the railway and the A380 (around the 1840s), because both the road and railway were built across the dairy company's land. All the land between the village and Scott's Bridge was the property of the company.

Toll-Houses

Before the A380 was built there was a toll-house at Penn Inn with a gate across the road coming down from St Marychurch Road into Newton Abbot. At the time when the A380 was built it must have been financed and constructed by one of the turnpike trusts.

The only other toll-house [Bill's] grandfather knew of in this area was on the road going towards Decoy at Langford Bridge Cross. The last occupant of that cottage was a man named Smale. It was vacated soon after 1904 when the farm almost opposite, Langford Farm, was run by two brothers named Bulley.

Closure of Toll-Roads

All of the toll-roads were taken over and the toll-houses sold off in the 1870s, when the roads were taken over by the Local Government Boards.

Quarry Stone

In his father's day and in Bill's own young days a lot of stone was required for making up the roads to give them a hard packed stone surface – no tar was used then. Most of the stone chippings were made by chaps getting the large rocks and crushing them by hand, but at the turn of the century a few (very few) private stone crushers were being constructed; there was one at Bickley Mill.

Stone from the Downs Quarry, where Foredown Kennels is now, was delivered on site within a reasonable radius at 2s.6d. a ton load plus a 1s.0d. for transport. The squire owned Maddacombe Quarry.

Stoneycombe Quarry

Bill talked at length about Stoneycombe Quarry and the roads serving it. The quarry was first opened in the 1840s and it was owned by the old South Devon Railway Company (SDR) which became the Great Western Railway (GWR). The only way to get stone out for the railways was by railway. They had built a substantial rail siding beside the main Newton Abbot–Plymouth line and for many years there were no roads serving the quarry. The quarry stayed in the ownership of the GWR for many years but not long before the First World War it was bought by the Mills family. During the First World War, POW labour was used for quarry work. During the time of Bernard and Jack Mills their assistant to the manager was Fred Crocker who with his wife trained the village children to do the maypole dancing for the fêtes. Most of the road haulage of quarry stone was carried out by the Vallance brothers who started work between the wars with horses and carts – only one to start with but it soon expanded with the large demands for road making, strengthening and surfacing. Soon haulage was done by lorries which brought their own maintenance problems in the early days.

The Vallances and Mills brothers then started making concrete blocks, mixing the concrete by hand, shovelling it onto wooden formers, waiting for it to dry and taking the formers away. They turned out hundreds like that. Eventually the Mills brothers sold the quarry out to English China Clays in the 1950s. All lorries coming to and from the quarry were weighed empty and full at the elevated weighbridge outside near the railway arch, but that soon went into disuse in the 1950s before the Mills sold it out.

Of course Stoneycombe Quarry is not in Kingskerswell as the parish boundary runs along the middle of the road outside the quarry. At one time the manager of the quarry was Joe Monkleigh who lived in the thatched cottage at the junction of Greenhill Road with Yon Street [see p16].

Village Refuse Pit

The refuse pit was in Churchway, about 200 yards from the junction with Greenhill, and had been an old disused stone quarry. The pit was used to dump village rubbish up to about 100 years ago. [This site is now covered with trees and on private land.]

Limekilns

Limekilns were about and being used quite a lot in Bill's young days and, of course, in his grandfather's and father's day. There was a limekiln on the left-hand side of the road near Barton Hall where Gypsy Small used to stop with his caravan. Behind Foredown Lodge there were two kilns in the quarry which were active right up to the 1920s. There was one in Church End Road, which was used for making the mortar for building in The Tors as well as other places. When the quarry was opened at Stoneycombe, either two or three kilns were built, then a few of the older and smaller ones closed when lime could be brought out by road. An awful lot of lime was used for 'whitewashing' walls inside houses as it was considered the best way to keep out flies, spiders, etc., and keep away germs. Outhouses, privies, etc., were 'whitewashed' at least once each year. At one time the interior of the Parish Church was 'whitewashed'.

Youth Movements

Bill said that in his very young days there were no

Scouts or Cubs and certainly no Army Cadets. He believed that the reason there were no boys' movements was because young boys were usually working for farmers, carters or anywhere they could make a few pennies.

There were Girl Guides run by a lady named Mrs Field who lived in Princess Road, and they were still going strong in 1947 when Bill left the village.

Unemployment was unknown in his father's time and his own young days. There were plenty of jobs and casual work for every man and, indeed, boy.

Choir

Bill Bovey was a boy chorister but left when his voice broke at 14 years of age. In his day the leading choirboy always sat in the box stall in front of the vicar's stall. Boys and ringers of the bells liked to attend weddings as they were each paid 7s.6d. for every wedding.

Bill's father was a bass in the choir but Reg Brinicombe and Bill Howard, also in the choir, were both tenors. Bill's uncle Henry Brooks and Bert Tanner were in the choir. Mr Sams the choirmaster, who was also headmaster at the school, gave up in the 1920s, and it was taken over by Mr Giles. After him Mr Birley became the next choirmaster.

Barton Hall

The squire closed Barton Hall in 1915 and came to live in 'Fluder House', but a 'rent' dinner was held in 1915 for all farmers and cottager tenants. Bill recalls that after the dinner each farmer was presented with a brace of pheasants and each cottager received a brace of rabbits. He did not know if this was an annual event.

The Revd Fagan

A great philanthropist in his parish, the Revd Fagan gave away almost all his life savings, and his stipend, so that he was not able to retire when he should have done. At 70 years of age whilst preaching a sermon at a morning service in 1924 he died very suddenly. [Cf. comment on Auntie Nance's version.]

Constitutional Club

Between the wars a committee was formed for the formation and building of a Conservative Club. The squire gave the ground on which the Club Room was to be built. Off his own bat, Mr John Banbury, a committee member, saw Lord Clifford of Ugbrooke and purchased the hall which had been used on the Lord Clifford estate for servicemen during the First World War. He paid £100 for the hall, and then told the committee what he had done. It was taken down at Ugbrooke and transported to its present site and erected.

Methodist Church

In 1911, Mr Whiteway built the present Methodist Church. The old one, now demolished, in Water Lane, was used by Mr French the butcher for storing wool. It was used occasionally to hold dances. Mr Whiteway also built the three cottages below the present Methodist Church in 1911.

Dance Band

There was a dance band in Bill's young days. At first it was just piano and violin and Mr Giles (organist) played piano and Bill played the violin. The band expanded as time went on. Bill's mother did all the arranging and the catering for the dances and for the whist drives. It all stopped in 1939 after Bill's mother collapsed with a stroke at a whist drive. She died three days later.

The 'Institute'

I asked Bill where the 'Institute' used to be. He told me it was what had been, until very recently, the Church Rooms in Daccabridge Road. It had been known as the Public Hall at one time before the new one was built on the main road. There had always been a flat 'attached' or in 'part of' the building, because his grandfather lived in the flat at one time. The upstairs room was used for dances, whist drives and socials, etc., before the billiard tables were put up in the big room.

Cider Press Lane

I enquired about the road where Pitt House is now. I believed it had been called 'Cider Press Lane'. Bill said that was correct, it got its name from the cider press by Pitt House. There was a road sign with the name of the Lane on it and it was demolished in the early 1920s when a steam lorry owned by Frank White coming from the quarry ran down over the bank and hit it. The sign was never replaced. That was probably at the time when Bob Fogwill occupied Pitt House.

Pitt House, Church End Road.

The Brown Family

I asked where the old squire used to park his coach and horses when he attended church, in Brook or Rose Cottages. No, in a building, since demolished, which used to be beside the north lych-gate. Bill said that old Langford Brown was very interested in shooting and fishing. He had a rather large caravan of the gypsy type

AROUND THE VILLAGE & PARISH

with four wheels and drawn by horses. Every year he had his caravan taken out to Runnage on Dartmoor, where he owned some shooting and fishing rights. It took up to four horses to pull it and the journey took a whole day, up to ten hours to arrive at the East Dart. [For the family's personal view on this event, Langford's wife Dorothy kept a diary, since published by The Devonshire Association as Family Holidays Around Dartmoor.]

Langford rarely rode a horse and rarely used a carriage; he used to walk to most places he wanted to go to, but he did use trains. During his lifetime he had the family burial plot in the churchyard railed off. Langford died in 1936 when Tom Brown took over the squireship, as Tom's father had died before Langford.

Bill explained the significance of the wall running across the woods between the Downs and Common in his young days, and in his father's too. People were allowed in the woods from the Downs side and where there is a gap in the wall with two large, rounded gateposts, there was an iron gate, always kept locked. The old squires, Hercules Langford Brown, and before him Hercules Edwin Brown, used the woods nearest the Common for breeding pheasants for their big annual shoots.

SOME GLEANINGS FROM SID GALE

The late Mr Gale was born in 1916 and for the first six months of his life lived in Coffinswell until his family moved to Kingskerswell, where he resided with his wife in Fore Street. An early memory of Fore Street outside the Gales' house was a pavement where it is rather narrow. Always ready for a chat, Sid and his wife would frequently be seen taking it easy sitting outside their front door – weather permitting of course. He married in 1941 but was then away in the war based in Palestine for four years. Sadly, he died in 2003. He recalled:

My father, who was Captain of the bell-ringers in the 1930s, planted willows by the brook in his garden, where Westcombe Motors used to be. There was a wooden bridge with a handrail over the stream. At the corner, off Coffinswell Lane, in those days was a small village green with a large hollow chestnut tree. It was about 1923/4 when at night-time an old lady called Aunt Sally would use it to go to sleep in. There were other itinerants who would go up to Zig-Zag Quarry in the evenings to cut ferns for their beds and then use the old pottery outbuildings down the lane leading to the present 'Barn

Above: *Fore Street from the junction with Daccabridge Road.*

Above left: *Gale's Greengrocers at the junction of Daccabridge Road and Fore Street.*

Left: *Fore Street, looking towards the Post Office.*

Left: *St Mary's Garage, Fore Street, 1952.*

Below: *Fore Street from the junction with Fluder Hill. Note the Devon Constabulary sign on No.67.*

Left: *Fore Street from the junction with Fluder Hill and Daccombe, Mill Lane, 2003.*

Right: *Fore Street from the junction with Fluder Hill, 2003.*

AROUND THE VILLAGE & PARISH

PC Hawkins' Constabulary with the Devon Constabulary sign above the door.

Owl', which used to be a farm, for sleeping. In the daytime these people would go to the Priory along the road to Abbotskerswell for soup and food.

Just up the road from our house, No.67 Fore Street was a police house. In the early 1920s PC Brock followed by PC Brawn were the village constables. The Fore Street station later moved to Broadgate Road.

Where 'Panorama' in Fluder Hill is now there was a farm with wooden sheds, owned by the two Miss Browns, Beatrice Grace and her sister Edith Clementina. Miss Beatrice looked after the cattle, three or four Guernsey cows, while Miss Clementina looked after the dairy side of the business. Both sisters lived in No.71 Fore Street and left the unpasteurised milk in the porch and villagers would come with a can, take a can full of milk and leave behind the can they had brought. My wife used to scald the milk to make cream as a special treat for our children.

The Misses Brown had 'Sedgewell' in Fluder Hill built and when foot and mouth was in the village they were able to move their cattle along the lane behind Sedgewell from their farm to field without putting them onto the road. Sedgewell at one time about the 1950s was a guest-house, before being purchased by Tony and Moira Mellor in the 1960s. They subsequently left in the late 1970s.

Further up Fluder Hill is a farm which at one time was worked by Farmer Mann and then by Mr Foss who moved from Rose Hill Farm in the village. Next to the farm are some terraced cottages, in one of which lived Andrew Lord who was gamekeeper at Barton Hall in the early 1900s. Andrew Lord used to preach at the Gospel Hall.

Fluder House was occupied by Mr Sears, a recluse. He was a talented artist who had exhibited at the Royal Academy. He used to grind his own pigments and mix his own paints, and used the barn at the back of Fluder House for all his drawings and art work. The next house on the left was called Trehurst. It stands back from the road and had a nursery garden owned by a Mr Howe in about the 1930/'40s. There were greenhouses, and goldfish in the tanks. Further on still, beyond the junction, was the limekiln.

As a lad in 1921, I went to the village school. At that time there was a school bell over the entrance. We sat five to a desk and there was a coke brazier for heating. One could look right the way up to the rafters of the high ceiling and it was often very cold in winter. Skipper England was the headmaster and used to sit with his feet up and read the Daily Express. There were three to four classes, with assistant teachers Miss Curtis and Miss Davis. The infants used to play opposite the school where houses now stand, while the older children's playground was where the present bungalow is, opposite the Scout Hall. The school used the greyhound track for sports days.

Prior to 1916, Miss Wale in Fore Street/Southey Lane ran a small private kindergarten in a wooden hut at the end of her garden. When the school closed, the St John Ambulance Brigade rented the hut and used it twice a week for training.

Across the road, Minnie Newbold in Southernhay had not been out for six years. As a young boy I would pick wild flowers with my friends, take them to Minnie, and she would give us a penny.

33

The baker Charles Hodge-Brooks on his cart going about his rounds with his horse 'Tommy'.

Opposite the greyhound track was Trevenn Farm owned by a Mr Gloyne. Before the Hare and Hounds was built, there was a highway and a big garden standing there. Lady Linden lived in Southey Lane and owned Claremont Estates. At the present bus stop at the end of Southey Crescent there used to be a cottage with a chestnut tree outside the cottage. This cottage, which was demolished for road widening, was owned by Claremont Estates and a gardener lived there called Nicks. Mortimore's had a shop opposite on the main road where I could buy five Woodbines for 2d. Nearby was a dairy called Jennings where now stand three shops, an antiques shop, a newsagent's and a Chinese take-away. The so called 'Manor House' further on was converted into flats in 1947. At the back it was all fields and a cowshed which was in what is now known as Manor Drive.

Mr George Mortimore, Mr George Brenton and Lou Blackmore were all bakers in the village. Mr Hodge-Brooks ran the shop opposite Fore Street at the top of Daccabridge as a bakery. His shop was later run by Mr Bob Fraser as a vegetable shop, and later still by my wife. We found an old oven when we took over the running of the shop. Next door to the existing Post Office was Bovey's bakery then run by Annie Bovey now aged 90, and adjoining, and round the back, was a taxi business run by Mr Petherick senr. There was a petrol pump and a petrol tank there for the purpose of the business. The other part of the Post Office was a butcher's shop run by Mr Fogwill. Also a Mo Lesley had a general store next to the Post Office. There used to be another Post Office in Vale Road, which closed in the 1970s.

In the courtyard of the Seven Stars on the old Kerswell Arch, I can remember there were tiled slabs with rings in for securing ponies or horses whilst their owners were having a drink. I particularly remember a Mr Sercombe, a portly gentleman who used to come in a pony and trap who, having imbibed generously, would need several people's assistance to get back into the trap. The pony would be given a sharp slap on the rump and would head for home which was at Compton. Next morning the pony, still harnessed to the trap with Mr Sercombe in it, would be found in his stable.

Fore Street.

AROUND THE VILLAGE & PARISH

Mortimore's

Above: *Mortimore's Bakery and Confectioner's, Fore Street.*

Olive May Mortimore with children Becky and Frank at the door of G. Mortimore's General Stores on Torquay Road, today Carter's Insurance Office.

Left: *George Mortimore, 1917.*

Right: *Mahala Mortimore.*

Right: *Postmen outside the Post Office, Fore Street, 1938.*

Left: *Fore Street with the Post Office on the left, 1952.*

Below: *Fore Street (now Garden Gate and the Post Office), c.1913.*

AROUND THE VILLAGE & PARISH

Where Ken Bedford, butcher, now operates were John and Frank Banbury, butchers. Mr Embury, also a butcher, was the first man to light the village street lights. He had his own generator and the lights were put on from 7.00–10.00p.m. I remember the village being gas lit in places and the lamplighter coming to turn the lights on. Mr Embury also once had a sheep with six legs!

In 1965 when Kerswell Arch was being taken down for the new bridge and road, small charges of dynamite had to be laid to bring it down, as the man in charge of knocking it down with ball and chain could not remove it.

In Brookador Cotts down by the stream lived Ned Causey and Mr Milverton senr, a coal merchant, whose coal yard was in Yon Street on the left-hand side before the new housing, formerly Crosslands Timber Yard. I worked for Mr Milverton two days delivering coal, two days delivering meat and two days delivering forage for cattle. Harry Butt and Bert Tapley at this time were stationmasters. Further on Pat Lovell ran a nursery on the right-hand side of Yon Street. At Whitpot Mill, Mr Birley would charge up accumulators for radios from his generator for people in the village.

Adams and Elliott, undertakers, had a rest room at the bottom of Daccabridge Road. In the 1930s a Mr Wyatt, who lived in Daccabridge Road, was a one-armed gravedigger. The old cider store in Daccabridge Road was at one time used for storing pantomime scenery. At the top of Daccabridge there was a working men's club in what later became the Parish Church Rooms and which is now two houses. Nearby, Roly Elliott's mother had a draper's shop. Where the present hairdressers is in Fore Street/Daccabridge Road was Spraggs' General Stores, later a fish-and-chip shop. The existing delicatessen was a sweet shop run by Miss Davies, later owned by Miss Causey who was a dress-maker. Mr Baldwin, who was a tailor, had a shop where the existing chemist now stands. Harry Paul had a shop there mending boots and shoes and he used to sit outside on the pavement.

I worked as a mechanic for three years for Mr Baldwin who had two lock-up garages. Opposite the Old Vicarage (now Midas' head office) was a draper's shop owned by Arthur Thorne and run by Peggy Neale.

Above and right: *Brookador.*

THE BOOK OF KINGSKERSWELL
Whitpot Mill

The wheel at Whitpot Mill Tea Gardens

Whitpot Mill, 2003.

AROUND THE VILLAGE & PARISH
Whitpot Mill

Ye Olde Whitpot Mill.

Below: Whitpot Mill Tea Gardens.

Whitpot Mill Tea Gardens, 1926.

Above and right: *Yon Street* with (above) *Jubilee Terrace*.

Below: *Vicarage Corner, Fore Street*.

Chapter 2

PLACES OF WORSHIP

ST MARY THE VIRGIN, KINGSKERSWELL

Despite not achieving parish status until 1828, the village of Kingskerswell has had its own church at least since the Norman Conquest in 1066, if not before. Domesday records a half virgate of land as being 'in the Church (lands) of this manor', an apparent gift of the Conqueror and Queen Matilda.

It would be most surprising if the village was without a church during the Saxon period before the Conquest in 1066. Significantly, the site of the settlement was directly linked to St Marychurch to the east. There are no known remains of an original Saxon church but, if indeed it existed, it would probably have been a relatively small thatched wooden structure standing on the same site as the present building.

The village's earliest known chaplain was William (family name unknown), in 1164, who came from the mother church of St Mary Church. The advowson eventually rested with the Dean and Chapter of Exeter. The close connection of church and manor has left the legacy of the Dynham family tombs in the church which were moved during a previous restoration, from their original chantry in the south side of the building, to their present resting place under the north-aisle windows. The three effigies are reputed to be of, first, Sir John Dynham (died 1428), recumbent in pointed helmet, mail, gorget and surcoat, displaying on his breast the arms of Dynham – *gules four fusils in fesse ermine*. A shield on the front bears the arms of Maltravers – *sable a fret or*. The second is of Sir John's first wife Eleanor (or Elianora, family name unknown), who died c.1394. She has supporting angels, with a wyvern at her feet. The highly decorated front is divided into compartments with niches containing the remains of saints and other figures, all badly mutilated. The third is of Sir John's second wife Maud, daughter of Sir John Maltravers of Hook, Dorset, and widow of Piers de la Mere. She died c.1410, without issue. The front panel of this effigy has either been cut away or plastered over, but the graceful recumbent figure lies with crossed hands, and her feet rest on a dog, an emblem of fidelity.

The earliest standing part of the church comprises the east wall of the chancel and the south transept, dating from the fourteenth century, along with the south porch and the massive tower. The north wall and north porch with parvis above were added about a century later. In addition to the effigies, there is some interesting ancient stained glass, fragmented but incorporated into several windows. Toothache sufferers can take comfort in St Appolonia who appears ready for action. The more contemporary stained glass is of some interest also; the east window glass of the Tree of Jesse was given in memory of the Revd G.H.F. Fagan by parishioners in 1925. Another window was installed in the south aisle in 1970 and commemorates William Adams. Long associated with the parish, Mr William Adams donated Church Meadow (Tithe Map name 'Pulley', or 'Poolhey', meaning water meadow), now a wildlife conservation area and the church car park. In 1889, the pulpit, from Bradford on Avon, replaced its very creaky wooden predecessor.

The early-fourteenth-century font was at one time replaced by another smaller one but was restored at a later date. The smaller font was offered to, and gratefully accepted by, the parish of Heart's Delight in Newfoundland, as documented by the Revd Fagan writing in the *Parish Magazine* in July 1894:

Referring as we have done to the work of the Church abroad, reminds us that the present is a good opportunity for mentioning what has become of a small Font which was for some time used in our Church, but afterwards banished to what is now known as the old Vestry. With the sanction of the churchwardens the Vicar offered it to the Revd G Johnson who worked for some years in Newfoundland and still has a son out there, and the offer was thankfully accepted. Mr Johnson wrote at the beginning of this year to say that the Font had at length reached its destination. He has given it to a new Church at Heart's Delight, while mentioning another Church that would be glad of it. He speaks of having four Churches to provide for, and though we have no more Fonts to bestow upon them yet he would be grateful, we know, for any Altar cloths or other Church material for which we have no further use.

In 1301 there were three bells. In 1815 five bells were cast by Pennington of Lezant in a nearby orchard, and parishioners were allowed to see the casting on

Left: *The Old Vicarage, Fore Street, built by the Revd Aaron Neck, now the head office of Midas Construction.*

Right: *The Church of St Mary the Virgin, Kingskerswell, looking west, c.1956*

Below: *The prospect eastwards over the Parish Church and railway bridge to the playing-field, 1997.*

PLACES OF WORSHIP

payment of sixpence. One of the bells is inscribed 'Peace and Goodneighbourhood', another 'William Neck & John Peckins CW', and a third 'Edward Adicott Kitson Vicar Aaron Neck Curate'. In 1887, Mr John Adams, Parish Clerk, noted that the fifth bell was cracked and had been in this condition for 30 years. He arranged the funding for recasting, Mr Henry Barter, a London merchant, giving £5.5s.0d., Hercules E. Brown Esq., JP, giving £10.0s.0d., and the Revd Walker, vicar, giving £5.0s.0d. The required sum of £45.0s.0d. was soon raised to pay Mr Aggett of Chagford for carrying out the work. In 1937 all of the bells were retuned and rehung, by Messrs Mears and Stainbank, of Whitechapel, London.

The rood-screen disappeared c.1847, when a few fragments were incorporated in the priest's stall; in 1931 the screen panels, now replaced before the entrance to the chancel, were found in Exmouth converted into a sideboard in the possession of the Revd Vaughan Stooke.

On 27 November 1946, a letter was received and published in the *Western Morning News*. It was written by the Revd C.G. Dawe, retired, and read as follows:

Sir, when I was Vicar of Kingskerswell, I came across an example of folk memory in a letter dated 1904, written to the Vicar at that time. The writer says, 'I left Kingskerswell in the year 1851, and I well remember the old Vicar, Mr Neck. He had lived all his long life in the neighbourhood and could tell many stories of old times. His grandmother, whom he well remembered, was born in the reign of Charles II, and she had told him how she had stood in the churchyard at Kingskerswell to see William III pass by on his way to Exeter when he first landed. She had also known a person who had been present at the death of Charles I.'

Revd C.G. Dawe, Cockington

William of Orange landed at Brixham on 5 November 1688 and marched to Forde House, Newton Abbot, on 8 November, passing the church on the way with his troops, which numbered between 30,000–50,000.

The Revd Aaron Neck was largely responsible for obtaining parochial independence for Kingskerswell. As recorded on his grave he, '... for fifty two years zealously laboured, the faithful and beloved minister of this Parish. Teaching the young, visiting the sick, and preaching the Gospel of God.' He established a new Vicarage (in 2003 the 'Midas' Head Office), a new parish school, and provided various furnishings for the church including a barrel-organ and new pews. His grave, with newly painted railings, is near the north lych-gate.

The Langford Brown family have also been significant benefactors. As lords of the manor for several centuries the family has maintained a long association with the church. Henry Langford Brown contributed also to the re-pewing with the Revd Aaron Neck. In 1875, Hercules E. Brown gave some land to extend the churchyard southwards, and Mr Thomas Hercules Langford Brown very generously donated the historic manor-house site held at the time of writing in trust for the parish.

Church End, c.1905.

View westwards across 'Pulley', now the church car park, with Squire Brown's coach-house in view and Church Cottages, at one time the parish poorhouse, to the right.

A view across Church Meadow with Foredown Farm behind, apparently nestling among the trees.

PLACES OF WORSHIP

Church interior, c.1940s.

For naughty people – the parish stocks, which are now in the church tower. Note the seven holes, suitable for three people and Long John Silver.

Vicars of St Mary Church, before 1828, Mother Church to Kingskerswell

1624	Robert Ball
1659	Robert Stidston
	William Reynolds
1683	John Campion
	James Salter
	James Salter
1767	John Feaver
1798	Edward Addicott Kitson
1827	George May Coleridge

Vicars of Kingskerswell

1828	Aaron Neck (appointed curate 1799) Grave Ref. 4/5/990.
1832	Aaron Neck licensed to Perpetual Curacy of Kingskerswell.
1852	William Balmborough Flower
1855	Charles Augustus Fowler
1859	George Morris, Grave Ref. 1/9/522.
1880	Augustine Harley Walker (Widow), Grave Ref. 1/2/122.
1889	George Hickson Feltrim Fagan, Grave Ref. 1/9/549.
1924	James Newland-Smith
1931	Clement George Dawe
1941	Alan Frederick Clifford Rowe
1970	Alan Raymond James
1989	John Francis Leonard

KINGSKERSWELL METHODIST CHURCH, WATER LANE

In about 1798 John Wesley's popular revival meetings in Devon and Cornwall roused some Kingskerswell residents to meet in their houses for prayer and worship. They eventually formed themselves into a 'society' which often met at Rose Hill Farm, since demolished, in the area of the modern-day Health Centre. By 1802 a small thatched chapel had been built in John Henley's orchard; this was followed by the purchase of a barn in Water Lane which was adapted and in use from 1827 for Sunday-evening services.

By 1898 the chapel was in debt, but Methodists in Torquay formed two mission groups to conduct street services under Mr A. Thomas and Mr F. Curtis, two local preachers, each on alternate Sundays. Within six months the chapel was cleared of debt. Continued missions held in the street between the Seven Stars and Lord Nelson Inn public houses recruited more converts to support the chapel, where a Sunday School was formed under Mr Fletcher.

Although still a struggling chapel, the decision was made to sell the old building and erect a new purpose-built one on a nearby site. So in April 1911 the foundations of the present Methodist Church were laid by Lady Layland-Barratt, followed by the building and subsequent furnishing in time for its opening in August the same year. A fresh start was made by the Sunday School, the pupils of which greatly enjoyed the local yearly outings.

Kingskerswell Methodist Church, Water Lane.

PLACES OF WORSHIP
Outings

*A happy bunch on a Methodist Church outing in the mid-1930s.
Left to right, back row standing: Marjorie Mitchell, Marion Jury, Daphne Towell,
Margaret Jury, Eileen Locke, Mavis Jury, Donald Honeywill, Mr Hayhurst
(Sunday School teacher), driver, Mrs Hartley, Miss Hayhurst, ?, ?, Katie Fletcher;
front kneeling: (partly hidden) Frank Vowden, Cyril Sampson, Betty Care, Mrs Sampson, Mrs Elliott;
front standing: Mr Honeywill, Mrs Honeywill, Mrs Wills, Mrs Hallett, Mrs Hawkins, Miss Nunn
(with dog), Mrs Mitchell.*

Methodist Church Sunday School outing, early 1920s.

United Reformed Church

Membership of the United Reformed Church in November 1898

Elizabeth Causey
Robert Croot
Emily Croot
Elizabeth Croot
Susan Drew
William Drew *(Sunday School Superintendent)*
Anne Field
John Freer
Elizabeth Freer
Wm Harvey Furneaux
Ann Furneaux
Bessie Ham
Thos Henry Harris
Elizabeth Harris
John Hart
Emily Hart
Mary Elizabeth Lord
James Mann
Esther Mann
Wm John Mills
Elizabeth Jane Mills
Bessie Rowe
Lydia Whiteway
James Yeoman
Mary Ann Yeoman

Also, by 1909:

Mr W. Hawkins
George Howard
Jessie Howard
Mr P. Jordan
Mrs E. Jordan
Mr A.E. Lock *(Deacon and Sunday School Teacher)*
Miss Luscombe
Miss M. Mills
Mrs Annetta Rowe
Mr Scobell
Mrs Scobell
Mrs Voysey

United Reformed Church, south window.

United Reformed Church, Yon Street.

By 1920 attendance was good, with a choir of 24 members, but despite a great deal of effort by many from Torquay who helped, led services and generally encouraged the chapel, the lack of direct ministerial leadership resulted in a slackening of interest and a decline in attendance. Nonetheless, sterling work by Mr Mogridge senr, Mr and Mrs Brooks and Mr R. Sellman not only aided progress but also led to the addition of a hall, kitchen, toilets and vestry. Continued efforts by Mr L.G.T. Mogridge (the chapel's historian) and others have enabled the furnishing of the chapel to be completed and have also helped to keep up numbers in the congregation.

For many years a thriving and active membership worshipped and met for many enjoyable social occasions. However, the more transitory nature of village inhabitants, combined with the departure of young people for employment elsewhere, have since led to the erosion of much of the structure which sustained this and other Christian groups.

Now for some years under the pastoral care of the Methodist Minister of Central Church, Torquay, the Methodist outreach continues, with the church secretary at the time of writing, Miss Grace Lacy, striving hard to continue the great tradition of effective work of Christian service and to maintain congregation numbers in the community.

KINGSKERSWELL UNITED REFORMED CHURCH

Kingskerswell United Reformed Church was built in 1854 by Mr Francis Man, as the 'New Room' in Yon Street, just outside the main village. It was registered as 'a place of meeting for religious worship' and its success caused Francis to extend the building in the following year. A Sunday School was begun, and when Francis died aged 59 in 1862, his widow Naomi had the hall and vestry added, then gave the buildings and land in trust for the use of the church and congregation, with the non-sectarian name 'Union Chapel' being introduced at this time.

Revd Henry Robinson became its minister in 1863, re-registered the building as a meeting-place for religious worship and for the solemnisation of marriages in 1866, while describing the congregation as 'evangelical protestant dissenters'. Revd Robinson died aged only 40 in 1868 and was buried in the church grounds with a headstone close by the footpath, the only burial on the site.

Revd Dowding then became the pastor but left five years later, at which stage the church became affiliated to the Upton Vale Baptist Church in Torquay, which partly funded evangelist Revd Priske to live in Kingskerswell.

It was Revd J. Joseph who in 1911 proposed the appointment of new trustees which included the secretary and treasurer of the Congregational Union. This done, Union Chapel became Kingskerswell Congregational Church, a name used for 60 years until the union of Presbyterian and Congregational Churches, after which the joint title of Kingskerswell United Reformed Church was adopted.

By 1932 all of the trustees had died, so new trustees were appointed, including Revd J. Seldon Whale, MA, Professor of Theology at Mansfield College, Oxford, later Principal of Cheshunt College. He had been a pupil at the Sunday School at Kingskerswell URC, where his mother was the church secretary for 19 years.

Changes in education, transport, and local development during the first half of the twentieth century meant that many of the younger inhabitants left the village to find work elsewhere, while many more adults with much smaller families moved in to settle. In the 1950s a deliberately accelerated village growth resulted in a large increase in the ratio of incomers to villagers; the last village-born URC member – Mrs Myra Milverton (née Causey) – died in 1995 after a connection with the church lasting 86 years. The church at the time of writing (a Grade II listed building) is conjoined to, and shares the minister of, another United Reformed Church in the Torbay District.

(PLYMOUTH) BRETHREN MEETING, TUDOR HALL

Thatched Tudor Cottage with now-blocked front entrance to Rock View. Kings Hill is in the foreground.

As their name implies, Tudor Hall and Tudor Cottage next to St Mary's churchyard were built in Tudor times when the Parish Church was enlarged by the Dynham family, then lords of the manor. The thatched roof was repaired and renewed not long before the time of going to press. Listed Grade II, the structure was known as Church House from 1566 to at least 1754. It is possible, even likely, that both Tudor Hall and Tudor Cottage initially provided housing for the construction workers, subsequently being used by parish officials and as accommodation for the visiting clerics from St Marychurch who had the service of this chapel of ease for many years.

It seems likely that Tudor Hall was the building mentioned in old documents as being in use as a schoolroom until the construction in the nineteenth century of the school on the corner of Dobbin Arch and School Road, the modern-day home of the Community and Leisure Centre.

After the school was built Tudor Hall became much less frequently used and, well into the twentieth century, it is believed that, through the Open Brethren Meeting at Prospect Hall in East Street, Newton Abbot, it was rented for meetings as an outreach to members living in Kingskerswell.

The entrance is via a side door alongside Tudor Cottage reached along a secluded side path. A delightful building with very thick walls and of simple construction, it has an air of quietness and restful tranquillity, oddly different from the troubled religious climate of the times during which it was built.

KINGSKERSWELL & THE RECHABITES

Looking through the deeds of my house, writes Janet Carter, I thought I had all the dates when the house was sold by Squire Brown after 1912, out of the Brown Family holdings in the village. I now find myself without a date for when the Faceys purchased the property. Mr George Charles Facey, a church bell-ringer and the captain of the bell tower for many years, died on 19 December 1953. His wife, Mrs Emily Jane Facey, died on 17 August 1959 and her executors assented to the vesting of three properties in her will, including 49 Fore Street to Mrs Margaret Louisa Prowse, and 51 Fore Street to Miss Monica Hocking.

When Mr and Mrs Facey lived at 49 Fore Street they offered the village the benefit of a 'Rechabite Temperance Society' run from this address, which ironically happens to be situated next door to the Lord Nelson public house. Many a Kingskerswell lad signed 'The Pledge of Abstaining from Alcohol' at 49 Fore Street, and many of those who signed stayed true to this and never touched a drop.

Stan Blackmore remembers being sent along to the society as a five-year-old in the late 1920s, thinking it was some sort of Sunday School or club. Stan, supping a pint at the Lord Nelson, reports that he never did sign the pledge!

Looking back, the late-nineteenth and early-twentieth centuries marked the golden era of temperance and prohibition, when an abundance of temperance societies sprang up, fuelled by the social consciences of the new middle classes, citizens who aimed at an improvement in the lot of the working masses. This they achieved by encouraging wage earners to desist from converting their hard-won pay into alcohol, and instead to take their money home to feed, clothe and care for their families.

Founded in 1835, the Independent Order of Rechabites was inspired by a passage found in the Old Testament, Jeremiah, ch.35. ('Rechabite' also refers to dwellers of round huts.) If the Methodist missions held in the street between the two public houses failed to recruit new members, then the Rechabite Temperance Society was equally ready and waiting for them. There is no doubting the benefits of the work of such movements, felt, in particular, amongst working-class families.

The scene at a fête in the early 1920s on the field now occupied by houses nos 1–4 Dobbin Arch. Note the piano on the haycart, the bell on the village school, the squeeze-box player and spectators all in Sunday best.
George Facey (right) is wearing his boater.

Chapter 3

MANORS

KINGSKERSWELL MANOR

On the day that King Edward the Confessor was alive and dead, in 1066, the manor was worth a hide and a half. As expressed in Domesday 20 years later, 'In the Church (lands) of this manor, is half a virgate of land.' A 'virgate', about 30 acres, was usually a quarter of a 'hide', a hide being, in the case of good land (measurements varied), about 120 acres. Since King William held one and a half virgates, and the villains held one hide, it would appear that the church's half virgate was a gift of the Conqueror and Queen Matilda, as already noted elsewhere.

The Saxon settlement site, effectively the nucleus of the manor, was strategically important, being beside the main ancient trackway, which crossed the marshes to the north and to the south at this point, from St Marychurch to various destinations westwards. This route followed the limestone ridge raised in primeval earth upheavals, which blocked the natural outlet of the River Teign to Torbay, and forced the river to divert east at Newton Abbot.

Long before the Saxons dwelt in Devon, however, this was an area of key human interest. A large late-Bronze-Age/early-Iron-Age field system and associated settlement, of which substantial remains are visible on the local limestone plateaux, is clear evidence of protected farming both within and without the parish boundary. A number of clear pieces of evidence also all testify to a long, continuous period of human habitation: a hoard of more than 2,000 late-period Roman coins, discovered in the mid-nineteenth century buried near the route westwards from the church and manor-house; the remains of a Roman habitation site north of the parish boundary; the Iron-Age fortified farm encampment at Milber; and the Iron-Age currency bars found in Coffinswell in modern times. Worked flints have also been found, within the parish boundary, suggesting an even earlier period of human activity.

Not to be ignored either are the Saxon personages of Dacca and Odda. Dacca's name is associated with the little bridge not far from the early settlement around the church and manor, and he may well be the same person after whom the mill and hamlet in Coffinswell are named. Odda's name is uniquely associated with the separate manor of Odicknoll (Odda's Knoll), in the south of the parish. Both carry the honour of being the earliest named local persons associated directly with a structure or property in the parish.

The settlement of the Cress Springs – Kerswell – was seen to be as important to William the Conqueror as it had been to the Saxon kings, both strategically and economically. William retained Edward's (and, of course, Harold's) Royal Manor in his own right, and the name perseveres.

Many of the lords of the manor down through the centuries have been identified. As a Saxon royal holding the manor was held by King Edward the Confessor and King Harold, passing, after the Conquest, to William the Conqueror, and then to Baldwin, Sheriff of Devon. He was followed by Sir John le Droun, who held it with the Hundred of Haytor, by the service of quarter a knight's fee, of the King. Next Sir John's son, Hamelin de Draiford, was the lord, after which the manor returned to the hands of King Henry II, who in 1156 granted it to the natural son of King Henry I and Sibella Corbet, namely Reginald, Earl of Cornwall. As he died without issue, the manor reverted to the King, who granted it to the Countess Dionisia, the Earl's daughter. After the Countess, by grant of King Richard I, it passed to the Earl's bastard son, Henry, Earl of Cornwall, who also failed to produce an heir.

On the death of Earl Henry in 1221, the manor remained with the King, and in 1230 King Henry III granted the manor along with the manor of Diptford and the advowsons of their churches for the service of half a knight's fee to Sir Nicholas de Moels. Thus was Nicholas rewarded for his part in the defeat of the King of Navarre. The name 'Moels' (which appears in several forms, including 'Molis' and, later, 'Mules') derives from Meulles in Normandy. Sir Nicholas may have been a relative of Baldwin the Sheriff.

Sir Nicholas worked hard for his holding, being called for military service many times, including a spell as Seneschal of Gascony. Two decades later, his son Roger received 70 marks from the Dean and Chapter of Exeter in exchange for the advowson of Kingskerswell. In 1338, Roger's great-great-grand-daughter (via his son Sir John de Moels, grandson John, and John's daughter Muriel Courtenay)

51

Left: *Foredown Farm, original Manor Barton. Note the apple orchard in the foreground.*

Below: *The view westwards over Pound House, now the Garden of Remembrance in the new churchyard. The scrub-covered De Moels-Dynham manor-house ruins stand in the orchard.*

Below: *Manor-house ruins, c.1914. The young lady, possibly A.W. Searley's daughter, is seated on a newel stair.*

MANORS

Manor-house ruins, c.1914.

brought both church and manor, by marriage, into the Dynham family.

The manor-house site, complete with 'romantic' ruins, and at the time of writing in trust to the parish by the generous millennium gift of the lord of the manor, is the subject of a lengthy investigation and consolidation programme. It seems very likely that the earliest phase of building was started by the de Moels at some time during the thirteenth century, if not before. The building shows evidence of having had a large hall, a separate kitchen and at least two storeys with newel stairs, reminiscent of Dartington in layout. The whole was aligned approximately north–south, and overlooked the vale towards Coffinswell. The manor pound would have been in view, off Pound Lane, the barton situated behind the main house to the west, with the Parish Church – resting place in the fourteenth and fifteenth centuries of several of the Dynhams – completing the prospect.

ODICKNOLL

The manor of Odicknoll lies to the south of the parish, near the Edginswell and Marldon boundaries. A separate history attaches to this manor, the name normally taken as meaning Odda's Knoll (see p51). There is no apparent specific reference in Domesday, and it is highly likely that the area was included, in some other guise, in another manor. However, Odicknoll covers rich agricultural and grazing land, the economic value of which would not have gone unnoticed. Modern-day civil boundary changes have split the traditional manor area between Kingskerswell and Torbay.

Odicknoll manor-house, nestling in the side of the 'knoll', looks east over the valley towards Fluder and is, at the time of writing, much altered, being a long, white, two-storeyed building with a slated roof, from which a stepped pathway leads down to the farm buildings and a lower lying walled garden. A covered spring issues from just behind the house and thence from a lower area before filling a pond, after which for a very short distance it forms part of the parish boundary.

The earliest recognisable reference to the manor is in a document of 1310 which includes the statement that John de Ferrers and Reginald de Remmesbiry held for one fee both 'Eggeneswell' and 'Odeknoll'. At some unknown date, the manor of Odicknoll became part of the holdings of Christchurch Twynham Priory in Hampshire. In 1553 the Priory's Odicknoll property was granted to John Ridgeway of Newton Abbot and John Petre of Hayes, Exeter. In 1538 the farm of the manor of 'Odicknolle' was leased for 84 years to a man named Thomas Wille, along with other 'appurtenances' in 'Odicknolle, Egeinswell and Southwilbergh'. Rent of property in 'Chamleigh' is recorded at the same time, and Chamleigh, the location of which is unknown, is henceforth linked as part of the manor of Odicknoll.

Mr Wille seems not to have had a good rapport with his son as the latter attempted to embezzle his father's deeds. Including Chamleigh, the 'clere yerelie valowe' of Odicknoll was £9.5s.8d. (Actually it was five shillings more, the Tudor scribe's arithmetic being very doubtful in accuracy.) The woods were designated at that time by John Graynfyld (general woodward for Devon) as being good enough only for repairs.

The farm seems to have been a substantial centre for cider production, as testified by archaeological evidence of the existence of a massive cider press (yet to be confirmed at the time of writing).

When William of Orange passed by, the area was used for a troop encampment, as was Milber Down north of the parish.

A more recent claim to fame was John Lethbridge of Newton Abbot. Mr Lethbridge spent much time and effort in his successful attempts to recover sunken valuables by means of a diving machine. The renown earned him commissions from many foreign governments and with the profits from these ventures he was able to buy the manor. The barton of Odicknoll was sold to Sir John Duntze, Bart., thence to the Wills family. The Tithe Map Apportionment of 1838 has Odicknoll house and garden with two adjacent fields in the ownership of Richard Tuckett and tenanted by George Luscombe.

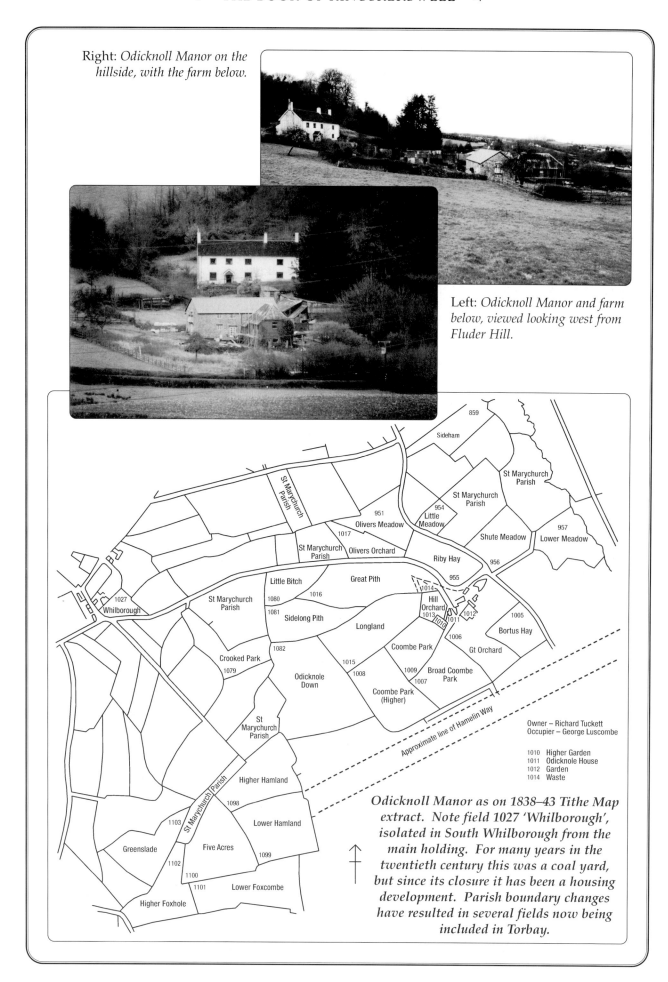

Right: *Odicknoll Manor on the hillside, with the farm below.*

Left: *Odicknoll Manor and farm below, viewed looking west from Fluder Hill.*

Owner – Richard Tuckett
Occupier – George Luscombe

1010 Higher Garden
1011 Odicknole House
1012 Garden
1014 Waste

Odicknoll Manor as on 1838–43 Tithe Map extract. Note field 1027 'Whilborough', isolated in South Whilborough from the main holding. For many years in the twentieth century this was a coal yard, but since its closure it has been a housing development. Parish boundary changes have resulted in several fields now being included in Torbay.

Chapter 4

THE RAILWAY

An early mention of the railway appeared in the *Torquay Directory* on 15 November 1848:

The Torquay Branch of the South Devon Railway is rapidly approaching completion, the permanent rails are laid as far as Kingskerswell and have been traversed by the engines conveying materials for the line which is to be completed in a few weeks.

In July 1849 a petition from the residents of 'Tormoham' (Torquay) for a station at Kingskerswell arrived on the boardroom table of the South Devon Railway. However, the directors stated that they would only agree to stop one train in each direction each day 'for a short time as an experiment'. This would have given very poor value for the expenditure, and the petitioners declined the railway company's offer. In 1852 a further request for a station was made, but turned down.

It had been intended that the railway, which has an incline of 1:110 going towards Torquay through Kingskerswell, would be run on atmospheric power, but this did not happen. The railway company in early 1853 had been approached for a goods siding in Kingskerswell, and this was agreed to, including a station as well. The land for the siding cost £25. The station opened for business on Friday 1 July 1853. Flags, flowers and evergreens decorated the branch engine that day, and great celebrations involving the firing of cannon, and sports, took place on a hill close to the new station.

The South Devon Railway had received a petition within days asking for more trains to stop on weekdays, but that a number might be reduced on Sunday evenings. This resulted in the Railway Board allowing two more up and down trains to stop on weekdays, and one less stop in each direction on Sunday evenings.

Kingskerswell Station in 1855, with single broad-gauge track and the junction to the new siding.

Above: *Kingskerswell Station, c.1905.*

Left: *Kingskerswell Station, c.1920.*

Below: *Kingskerswell Station, c.1920, showing the entrance to the ticket office and no footpath on the exit to the road.*

THE RAILWAY

There was a case of vandalism on 14 May 1856, when:

... a large cable used for drawing carriages from the side rail at Kingskerswell was maliciously thrown across the main line. The up express passed over it at full speed and was badly shaken.

A collision took place at Kingskerswell on Saturday 19 November 1864. A special goods train with six or seven trucks left Newton for Torre at 8.30p.m. In failing to stop at Kingskerswell, it ran on into the section at Torre and collided with the 7.55p.m. from Kingswear. This resulted in a second- and a third-class carriage on the train both being derailed; several passengers on the second-class coach were bruised and shaken.

It was reported to the directors of the railway, on 22 January 1874, that the '9.15a.m. up train was derailed at Kingskerswell in consequence of Porter Moore being asleep – Fined 2/6d.'

In August of the same year the board of the South Devon Railway approved the doubling of the broad-gauge track to Kingskerswell.

Taken from a local paper, the train timings for 1875 showed that departure from Newton Abbot to departure from Kingskerswell took an average of six minutes.

Good progress was being made in doubling the line between what is now Aller Junction and Kingskerswell. The *Torquay Directory* recorded that the double line from Newton to Kingskerswell was opened on 22 May, although no official confirmation of this exists, and the South Devon Railway timetable dated 1 July 1876 showed only one train at a time between Newton Abbot and Kingskerswell. It appears that a second platform was provided at Kingskerswell in 1876. In 1880 the Great Western Railway decided to double the three miles, 32 chains between Kingskerswell and Torquay at a cost of £14,300, including alterations at Torre. A local paper reported the double line between Kingskerswell and Torquay being used for the first time on Sunday 26 March 1882.

By 1883 there was a new signal-box at Kingskerswell, which had 13 levers and four spare. A report made by a GWR general manager, which was considered by the board on 2 March 1891, mainly covering the 'narrowing' of the gauge, included an allowance for Kingskerswell of £686 for the extension of the siding and provision of toilets.

Included in an inspection by Colonel Yorke, on 27 July 1911, were the extended platforms at Kingskerswell. These had been doubled in length at the Kingswear end to 600 feet, at a cost of £1,719.

Authority had been given for the station to be re-equipped with gas lighting instead of oil, but this may have been postponed as electric lighting was installed in 1922.

The station had several unusual features, the main one being that it had a two-storey building on the up platform, giving access to the road which was higher than the platform. The booking office was on the first floor, with two flights of stairs down to the waiting-room on platform level. There was another ladies waiting-room on the platform. The up platform also had a gents toilet and a small Saxby and Farmer signal-box containing 17 levers. The siding was on the Torquay end and could hold 22 wagons. Towards the end of the era of steam, this siding was observed being used by a tank engine and wagons which were being employed to put gravel on the Torquay end of the down platform. Between trains the points were switched to cross tracks and trains waited in the siding. The down platform was accessed by a wooden stairway from the road and the waiting-room had doors at the front, with windows. During the summer, passengers would use the waiting-room before catching the train to Goodrington where they headed for the beach.

Several Royal Trains have passed through Kingskerswell, one example being on Tuesday 8 May 1956 when an empty Royal Train, the 11.15a.m. Barnstaple Victoria Road to Goodrington, went through being hauled by two highly polished Castle Class locomotives, numbers 7024 Powis Castle and 5044 Earl of Dunraven. The train later left Torquay at 11.00p.m. for Grampound Road in Cornwall.

On Wednesday 27 March 1963 the *Herald Express* published details of the Beeching Report. The main headline read 'Three South Devon Stations Under The Beeching 'Axe", continuing:

Plan urges 'revolution' that hits West holiday towns. Three South Devon railway stations are among a total of more than 2,000 which the Beeching Report, published today, recommends shall be closed. They are those at Kingskerswell, Churston and Dartmouth.

Kingskerswell signal-box closed on 28 September 1964 at the end of the summer season, the station losing its passenger services on 5 October the same year – it was the only station on the line to do so. It is interesting to note that Churston Station is still in use today and that Dartmouth Station building still stands.

In 1968, a group of Torquay schoolboys completed a survey of the line as part of a school project. This included the following:

KINGSKERSWELL; The Ticket Hall and Waiting Room form a two storey building on the up side with outside access at first floor level. There are two flights of stairs from the Booking Office to the waiting room at platform level. There is another Waiting/Ladies Room on the platform.

Their observations can be seen in Torquay Reference Library, and form part of a valuable historic record.

The building had been completely demolished by April 1968, although the platforms are still in place in

57

Left: *Engine No.5558 travelling towards Kingskerswell, with Scott's Bridge in the distance. This view has suffered radical changes during the latter half of the twentieth century. The 'Toby Jug' houses on the left have gone, and a major roundabout has appeared, along with a new bridge which routes the road through a field on the right. Before boundary changes, the hillside on the left fell within the parish boundary.*
© Peter Gray

Right: *Engine No.5074 passes through Kingskerswell Station and the seven-arched railway bridge, 4 July 1958. The engine worked down 'Torbay Express' to Kingswear, before returning with 'Goodrington' to Newton Abbot goods yard.* © Peter Gray

Left: *Kingskerswell passengers waiting for the 3.03p.m. resign themselves to a further wait as Engine No.3854 trots past with a holiday relief (c66) at 3.06p.m., on 5 August 1961. Their train, the 9.55a.m. from Swansea, arrived at 3.31p.m.*
© Peter Gray

THE RAILWAY

2003, albeit with partial covering vegetation. The signal-box, goods siding buildings, waiting-room and down-platform stairway have gone, as has the two-storey station building; stone has been pushed under the seven-arched road-bridge archway where it once stood. The road-level access points to the station building and down-platform stairway have been blocked in.

There has been much talk of reopening the station, and with good reason. Situated within the village, with platforms that were well built still in place, such a move would represent a big cost saving. There is potential use of St Mary's Church car park, only a short distance from the Newton Abbot end of the up platform. The creation of a direct pedestrian access to this platform from the car park would present few difficulties, and even a footbridge access from platform to platform could be built. Kingskerswell Station used to be a very well maintained asset for the community, and it is the view of many that with a little foresight and imagination it could well be so again.

A 1950s view of the 'Torbay Express' holiday train passing the Parish Church.

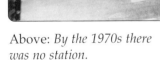

Above: *By the 1970s there was no station.*

Above right: *The seven-arched bridge, with six arches in this view which has since become obstructed by a building development.*

Right: *Bird's-eye view of the old station yard in the days when it was used for light commercial concerns. It is now a housing development.*

59

Mary Bulley's cottage, Abbotskerswell.

Below: *The Lord Nelson Hotel, Fore Street.*

Below: *May Day parade outside the Lord Nelson Hotel, Fore Street.*

Chapter 5

THE PARISH COMES OF AGE

ASPECTS OF PARISH LIFE IN THE 1890s

Village life in the 1890s revolved to a large extent around the parish of St Mary's and its central charismatic figure, the Revd Fagan. The *Parish Magazine* was launched in January 1890, priced at 1d. a month! Issues from the first decade in the life of this publication provide a revealing and often entertaining insight into what was an important period of change, with the transition from an ecclesiastical to civil authority, as well as the conduct and management of local affairs.

During this time schooling was a matter for the parish, not, as today, the local authority. The existence of the school relied to a large extent on voluntary contributions from the wealthier members of the parish, the Government grant paid each year being dependent on the report of the annual school inspection! On 1 September 1891 the managers of the Kingskerswell National School abolished fees, making voluntary contributions an even more important item in the school accounts.

During the last week of school fees the attendance averaged, in the large school, 69 out of a possible 81, and in the infants' room, 51 out of 69. In the November 1891 issue of the *Parish Magazine* there appeared the following comment:

We hope that nothing more than the weather has been the cause of the bad attendance during the last month, surely the new broom 'free education' is not beginning to wear out at this early stage of its career?

In May 1893 it was reported that the Education Department required the school to be enlarged as 130 children were using a room thought fit for only 112! It was agreed to build a new infants' room on the back of the existing building and a fund was established in order to finance its construction. The Infants' School, built at a cost of £376, opened in September 1894 and was a success:

The attendance has been very good, although blackberries seem rather an attention. We would point out to parents and children that the school will commence at 1.30 instead of 2.00 for the next few months, so that there will be ample time for blackberry picking after school hours.

October 1894 saw the commencement of a Night School for young men (Evening Continuation School), geography, history and mensuration being taught to 49 students in the first month. In 1895, classes for young women were started and lessons in cookery and carpentry introduced.

The Arts and Crafts exhibitions of June 1891 and Easter 1892 were direct spin-offs from the 'technical and cottage art classes' started by Mr Phillips of Aller Vale Pottery fame. These exhibitions ensured for Kingskerswell (and also for the neighbouring villages of Abbotskerswell and Coffinswell) a degree of celebrity reaching far beyond the confines of the parish boundary.

During the 1890s it was necessary to close the children's schools on two occasions due to an outbreak of scarlatina and, in 1898, whooping cough.

The parish had its own library, books being exchangeable at the National School Room every Sunday, after the afternoon service. Subscribers paying 1d. per month were entitled to one volume at a time, those subscribing 2d. per month to two volumes!

Reference is made to the 'Fire Relief Fund' in September 1890, although regrettably when and where this fire occurred is not mentioned. It was ascertained that the total loss suffered by those affected by the fire amounted to £260, compared to the total sum collected of £125.3s.0d. Consequently a distribution of 9s.3d. in the £ was made.

A party of parishioners, including the squire, the vicar, the overseers and the parish officers, assembled outside the Lord Nelson Inn on Monday 6 October 1890 at 8.00a.m. for the purpose of perambulating the boundaries of the parish ('beating the bounds'). On this the *Parish Magazine* reported:

The route taken was of course the parish boundary line, wherever it chose to take itself, and it was taken by the great majority of those who were at the start, a fact on which we pride ourselves. The place of starting was reached again at about 4.00 p.m. after a halt at Browns Bridge, where the Squire most generously supplied refreshment, and a supper at the Lord Nelson at which Mr Brown presided, concluded the day's proceedings.

It was also reported in November 1890 that the

61

widening of the Water Lane approach to the village had 'every prospect of being realised, and that before winter is over visitors to Kingskerswell as well as inhabitants will be struck with the great improvement which will have been made.' This work was completed in 1891 at a cost of £80, the expenditure again being met by local contributions.

The parish was also responsible for the lighting of the village, which was paid for by public subscription to cover the cost of oil and lighting from October to March. An additional lamp was installed in Daccabridge in 1897 and a further three, including one for the school, in 1898.

Voluntary contributions helped with the cost of coal for distribution to the needy at Christmas and the monthly Clothing Club had almost 100 members, those paying on a regular basis being entitled to an annual bonus of 2s.6d., partly paid for by local subscription.

These voluntary contributions were frequently made less wearing on the pocket through the staging of many 'Pleasant Evenings' – entertainments of an 'in-house' nature and often taking the form of a presentation of choral and dramatic elements organised by, for example, Dr MacDonald and Miss Penny.

The troublesome question of the parish water-supply arose on a regular basis and in March 1893 a special meeting of the parishioners was called by the overseers at the request of the Newton Sanitary Authority. It was explained that a sum likely to exceed £3,000 would be needed to pay for the works contemplated, repayable over 30 years. It was finally agreed, in 1898, that Torquay Corporation would supply Kingskerswell with water, and, on 14 August 1899, work commenced on the excavation of the reservoir, the first stage of the works costing £2,064. All houses were charged 1s.6d. in the pound per annum on the rateable value and the sum of ten shillings per annum for each bath. The rules were clear:

No person shall be permitted to draw water from a private tap for which he or she does not pay a water rent under the penalty of a £5 fine for each offence and any person allowing water to be drawn from his or her tap by any other person will be liable to the same penalty of £5.

In 1897, to celebrate Queen Victoria's Diamond Jubilee, numerous events took place, including a 'Trades Procession', some 26 entrants strong, and a feast on the Downs:

As we gazed at the piles of bread and cakes, and watched some of those who had worked the hardest staggering under the weights of the rounds of beef, we said 'sure there'll be grub enough' and yet it must be confessed that there had to be carving to the bone, and that before tea was over 'cake there was none'.

Ample supplies of ale, cider and aerated waters slaked the thirsts of all who attended. Dinner over, the sports committee organised events for young and old, including a one-mile race, sack race, egg-and-spoon race for women, putting the weight and tug of war. Those with enough energy could dance the evening away at the Institute or attend the bonfire which was duly lit at 10.00p.m. in a field near Fluder.

Sufficient monies were also collected to install permanent seats on the Downs, costing £10, and a commemorative clock was added to the church tower, at a cost of £111.

ROYAL ALLER VALE POTTERY, KERSWELL'S MOST CELEBRATED INDUSTRY

Royal Aller Vale Pottery was situated on the northern edge of the village of Kingskerswell but within the parish of Abbotskerswell and had been so for centuries. After the pottery had closed and the Second World War had passed, the site became a small housing estate. This isolated eastern outpost of Abbotskerswell was incorporated into Kingskerswell when the Diocese of Exeter, by Act of Parliament, rationalised the situation by using the main railway line to Plymouth as the boundary for the two parishes.

Broken tiles of the medieval style found in Haccombe Church have been excavated from this site. In 1868 the small pottery was leased by a clay merchant from Newton Abbot, named John Phillips. He was born into a family at Shaugh Prior which had a brick-making and clay-mining business there as well as being distributors of clay at Newton Abbot. John, quite clearly influenced by William Morris, founder of the Arts and Craft Movement, was instrumental in founding cottage classes in the villages of the Aller Valley and the Newton Abbot area.

An art exhibition mounted by the Newton Art Schools in 1881–2 so fired his imagination that he determined to bring beauty into the everyday life of the villagers of the Kerswells. Aided in particular by his sister Elizabeth and Dr Symons, his classes were intended to teach skills to the young uneducated folk who in those days had little expectation of life except drudgery.

At Kingskerswell they met in the Gospel Hall but in the two other villages these were true cottage classes, and lessons took place at Mary Bulley's home in Abbotskerswell and at John Easterbrook's cottage in Coffinswell. In his address to The Devonshire Association in Tavistock in July 1889, John Phillips described with conviction his rationale, and the serious purpose and 'fun' aspect of the early classes:

Our young villager, when he has passed the 'standards' that sapient legislators have set up for his confusion, reckons that he has finished with

THE PARISH COMES OF AGE

Arthur Pearse as a young man at Royal Aller Vale Pottery.

'zaminations' for the rest of his days; and if in any form such an abomination is presented to his notice, 'not if he knows it' will be his sentiment, and a suspicion of such things ever hangs around the doors of the schoolhouse. Circumstances beyond our control placed the board school in our village of Abbotskerswell out of convenient reach, and we were thus driven into a cottage that was kindly placed at our disposal. This proved to be the crowning of the edifice. No odour of 'standards' hung around its rose-covered walls, no 'scent' of 'zaminations' was found to be secreted in the thatched roof that covers the cottages of Mrs Bulley and her neighbour, John Brimblecombe, nor hanging about the entrance. Set out with trestle-tables and 'stools' brightly lighted, and with the cheerful blaze of a log-fire, the 'Art School' invited our young people to a 'pleasant evening.' Twice weekly have twenty-five of them, ranging from eleven to twenty-three years of age, met in this cottage during the past winter. Freehand and coloured drawing became immediately attractive; their designs were worked out and applied at home on wood, copper, brass, ironwork, and needlework. In this last the endeavour was to bring suitable decoration in colour into the cottage homes of the village; a design was worked out in the school for the half curtain of the cottage window, and then carried out in the house on the cheapest of muslins with highly satisfactory results. The ironwork has brought fame and profit to our village smithy, and the parish church of Kingskerswell is adorned with wrought iron lanterns that contain the lamps for lighting the church, made by our village blacksmiths. The decoration of pottery has given regular employment to a number of young villagers, and the wood carving has brought an order from the Princess Louise for a carved chest 'after' the old family chest of Churchwarden Vening. Mr Vening's family have farmed their own freehold estate in this parish [Abbotskerswell] for the last four hundred years. Visitors to our Cottage Art School have been greatly entertained and interested by the bright and merry group of young people who greeted their entrance. It has been a frequent custom to close the evening with glee and song and chorus. For this use a special book was arranged, containing such songs and ballads as 'The Farmer's Boy,' 'Hearts of Oak,' &c., and a special song written for the three villages that are united in this work, and which I append to this paper.

Altogether 64 young people attended, ranging in age from 11–23, and they not only made pots but carved in wood and stone, painted, stitched and embroidered and were taught ironwork by the village blacksmith.

Kingskerswell lads made wrought-iron lamps for the church and Princess Louise opened an exhibition of their work in Torquay. The Princess autographed a model for Sam Main, who, together with many of his fellow pupils, went on to work with Phillips at his Aller Vale Pottery. When Collard opened the Crown Dorset Art Pottery in Poole, Sam moved too and kept his own distinctive mark with the inscription 'Sam made it' on the bottom of each pot.

Left: *Fore Street from the junction with Barnhill Road, looking towards Daccabridge Road with Marguerite Way on the left.*

Right: *Fore Street from the junction with Barnhill Road, 2003. Marguerite Way can be seen on the left.*

Below: *Fore Street looking towards the Barnhill Road junction.*

THE PARISH COMES OF AGE

Princess Louise, Marchioness of Lorn and daughter of Queen Victoria, was not only a passionate follower of the Arts and Craft Movement but was also a frequent visitor to South Devon where she regularly came to stay with friends in Torquay. While in the area she would often give her support to local exhibitions of the arts. In 1886, the Princess visited the Aller Vale Pottery after purchasing some of its products. This began a very long connection of patronage which was often blessed by requests from the Princess for Aller Vale to exhibit in London displays where she was the patron. Thus it was that the prefix 'Royal' was granted to the company.

The result of this interest was acclaim indeed. Other members of the Royal family became customers, including Alexandra, Princess of Wales, later to become Queen Alexandra, wife of King Edward VII, and some later design styles had names such as Sandringham and Princess Wares.

In 1889 a 27-year-old Italian decorator named Domenico Malpucci, from the Farina Pottery near Florence, came to the Royal Aller Vale Pottery as a full-time instructor. He had also worked at some of the London studios before coming to Kingskerswell.

In 1891 he lived with his 24-year-old Italian wife in Hillside, the large house on the corner of Fore Street and Barnhill Road.

Another prominent name at the Pottery was that of John Skinner from Mid Devon, who as a youngster worked in the potteries of Staffordshire. On returning to Devon he came to the Aller Vale Pottery where, because of his skills and willingness to help others, he was given a job alongside John Phillips in the cottage art classes, teaching the young. John Skinner lived in Main Street, now Fore Street, Kingskerswell. After John Phillips' death, many of the staff left the company and so it was that John Skinner found himself a director of Longpark Pottery in Torquay.

At one time as many as 70 people were employed at the Royal Aller Vale Pottery, and many of their surnames are still to be found in and around Kingskerswell to this day; (George) Bond, (Ernest and Louis) Brimson, (Frederick) Cockram, (Thomas) Causey, (Samuel) Hicks, (Thomas and William) Burn – all of which are recorded in the 1891 census. Albert Elliott, of Fore Street, made or decorated the vases presented to Princess Louise at the 1890 Torquay exhibition.

Song of the Three Wells!
A Swiss air, written for the Cottage Art Classes

WHEN stars shine bright, And Cynthia's light Falls gently over hill and plain;
When hushed to rest Each quiet nest, And shadows deepen in the lane,
Then comes the hour, the mystic hour, When Arts and Crafts assume their power,
In Coffinswell! and Kingskerswell!
And so in Abbotskerswell too!
For here we merry craftsmen dwell,
And wondrous is the work we do!

This county blest, That in the West, Lies softly 'twixt the balmy seas;
In days of old, As we are told, Was famed throughout the world, for these
Our Arts and Crafts, which here we ply When winter nights go swiftly by.
(Refrain)
Should storms assail, Or floods prevail, We speed across the rugged ground;
For in our lore 'Tis reason more, That at our trysting-place we're found;
Thus helping on, with heart and hand, The glory of our native land.
(Refrain)

E.P. (Elizabeth Phillips)

Mrs Radmore, School Road, relaxing in Church Meadow, c.1930

Above: *Kit Warman.*

Left: *Kit Warman, the first Kingskerswell postwoman, photographed during the First World War.*

Chapter 6
VILLAGE LIFE RECALLED

AN 'VACUEE' IN OLD KINGSKERSWELL

There follows a memory or two of old Kingskerswell which people may have forgotten, one of which is that this has always been a very good limestone-producing area; the very large Stoneycombe Quarry tells us this. For years before that, this stone was dug out in quite a few places around the village in fairly small areas, each with a limekiln to burn the stone and produce powdered lime which was used for all kinds of things. A few of these kilns are still here, if you know where to look. The first one that I know of is situated at the higher end of

Nos 47–49 Daccabridge Road, before renovation and after damage by vandalism, c.1947.

Nos 47–49 Daccabridge Road, after renovation.

Churchway, on the right in a field, near a few trees and an outcrop of rock. People lived there for many years in a caravan. A well is close by. [This kiln site has since been infilled, earthed over and returned to pasture.]

Another kiln can be found in what is now the Kennels at Foredown Lodge, close to the small quarry behind it. The kiln has now been covered and built into what is a workshop type place. A third one, and it is a very good one, was oddly built, with the large centre key-stone of the arch being misplaced in building – or the whole arch has moved somehow. This kiln is also now built into a garage so is out of sight. It lies in the garage of 'Tudor Cottage', by the churchyard. One can see behind it, in the next cottage garden, where the rock was removed and now forms the garden. [A large house has since been built on the garden.]

The other one that can still be seen, but [which] is really grown in although almost on the roadside, is on the Kerswell Road, nearly up to Barton Hall, just past the lane on the left that leads down to Daccombe. One would have to search a little to find it. These are a few of the old kilns of interest. If anyone would like to have a look, permission would have to be asked for from the owners.

At the lower end of Daccabridge Road, there is a large size barn, which is now just an old building used as a store. This building used to be a wine and cider store, and pound house for making cider, etc. It had two or three levels of floor, and I believe a hoist was used to get the barrels up above. In fact, about 30 years ago, I was sent down to the building by its then owner to cut out and remove the large floor joists, and also cut up the remaining few hogsheads, or barrels. These were of a size large enough to get inside! A lot of wine. I was offered the barn for a youth club in the village, which two of us ran for a year or two, until outside elements ruined it for us.

Also above this building and behind it, in 'Gara Lodge', in a large room, or area behind and underneath the house, was a wine storage place. The walls were joined to a floor which was curved up into the walls. This it seems was for ease of storage and cleaning. We found this when working on it, to convert it into the doctors' surgeries, when they moved from The Tors to the village. Mr Wally Maggs who owns the house, and had the conversion carried out, would be able to explain more...

67

While on the subject of Lower Daccabridge I must mention the two cottages, Nos 47 and 49 which are at the bottom of that road as it leads into the playing-field. As a result of continued vandalism, the cottages were converted in 1975/6. The end cottage had to be demolished by order of Newton Abbot District Council. When I converted these into dwelling-houses, I discovered that they were built in about 1749, and there was a Preservation Order on the small building and chimney stack – only ivy to be removed. A 2oz copper penny (cartwheel penny 1749) was found set in the bottom of a door frame, thus dating the cottages. A coin was set like this, or in a window-sill, to date the building in years gone by. The penny was the first copper coin to be made in place of silver hammered coins. These particular coins were not used for long as they were too heavy. The attached small barn was used as a laundry about 100 or more years ago, and is now garages. Side on to the above were four outside privies for the cottages.

I wonder if many remember that at Aller Cross on the old Newton Road, in the grounds behind the big house on the corner, there used to be a car breaker's yard, during or after the Second World War.

I also wonder if people remember, or if they themselves ever used, a right of way footpath that ran from Huxnor Cross, opposite the 'phone box into the gate of Dellside Cottage down the path, now a driveway through the garden and steep bankside, over a stile in the rear hedge into the fields, and across to Churchway Lane, where it widens out about three-quarters of the way along it quite near the limekiln? Of course it is now closed because it was never used for many years. I lived next door for many years. It is the only place I know of in the 'Kerswell area where the nightingale can be heard singing at night down the valley, by Churchway Lane.

As one travels past the Bickley Mill Inn down in Stoneycombe valley on the way to Compton, the road forks, and in between the two lanes lies a quite large marshy copse [now strictly private]. Does anyone, like me, remember when up to 50 years ago, that whole area was a small lake? It was full of water fowl and great for we kids; it was teeming with tadpoles, newts or some kind of fish. My friend's dad had three Indian type canoes, which we used to have great fun in on this water. Our pleasures in those days were simple.

Did anyone ever play putting on the green down in the playing-field (down the swings end), that so many of us worked so hard to make and get under way. It went the same way of so many things. [There was] no interest to help, only [to] play!

Well, these are a few things of the area, of years ago, and I dare say that it has been thought of already. I notice now, that I seem to have told a little tale of most things, so I will stop here. I hope it may be of interest, or ring a bell for some folks. There are so many tales of people, places and things I seen and done all my life in Kingskerswell... and I, Alan Davies, am only a 'vacuee' in the war!

Auntie Nance, April 2003

My name is Annie Marsh Adams and I was born on 21st October 1911, at 3, Fore Street, Kingskerswell. Dr Rayner Hatfield delivered me at home, he was the local doctor who lived at Pen-y-Craig, The Tors. Mrs Hatfield started the first library for children there and kept books in amongst the medicine bottles. We would walk over there after Sunday School to change our books.

I was the youngest of four children born to Ellen (née Hodge-Brooks) and Alfred Lang Bovey. I had two brothers, William (Bill) and Charlie, and a sister, Dorothy.

My mother was born at Kismet, Fore Street, Kingskerswell, on 11th November 1870. She was the third of 13 children born to Martha (née Marsh) and William Hodge-Brooks who was a fishmonger. My father was born at Sharpham Manor, Ashprington, where his parents were coachman and cook. He bought the land at 3, Fore Street from Mr Crocker the butcher (Jabez Petherick's great-uncle) who lived next door where the Post Office is now. It was then a butcher's shop with a slaughterhouse around the back. When I worked at the Post Office Mr Bloxham (senr) often went down to the cellars when they flooded to clear away animal bones.

Above: *The Bovey family. Left to right, standing: William, Charles, Dorothy; seated: Ellen (née Hodge-Brooks), Annie Marsh, Alfred Lang Bovey.*

Left: *Annie Marsh Bovey.*

VILLAGE LIFE RECALLED

Above: 'Tommy', waiting patiently outside the Seven Stars Inn, for his owner, Charles Hodge-Brooks, who is inside. Note the bread on the cart. The card is postmarked 26 July 1909.

Left: *The Hill family: Fred Hill, Great Granny Hill, Silas, Gwen and William.*

The Garden Gate was a grocer's/Post Office and I remember they used to keep salt fish in the attic to keep it fresh and cool. Dad was a baker at Callards but he decided to build his own bakery and house on his land so he could marry my mother. Meanwhile he left Callards and baked bread in an oven at Bickley Mill. They married in Kingskerswell church on 15th July 1901. The vicar came from St Michaels Church, Pimlico, Torquay, because Mum (Ellen) was in service in Torquay.

I was christened by Revd Fagan. My Godfather was my uncle Charles Hodge-Brooks who drove a horse and cart delivering bread and cakes around Kingskerswell, Coffinswell, Daccombe and Whilborough. The horse was called Tommy and he is pictured on a postcard with Mr Andrews who had a retarded son called Bill and lived in the cottage opposite the church backing on to the Coach House. Charlie lived and worked with us at the bakery, he was engaged but the girl died. About 1914 Gertrude Mary Goad from Yealmpton came to teach at Kingskerswell School. They married and he served on HMS *Foresight* and later lived at 26, Fore Street where they ran a grocer's shop and taxi service.

My Godmothers were Charlotte Mitchell (my cousin and Bert Mitchell's aunt) and my aunt Matt (Martha) Gully (née Hodge-Brooks) who ran the New Inn at St Marychurch. My aunt Jess Milton (née Hodge-Brooks) ran the old Seven Stars on the bridge, and her second husband was George Causey, a director of Longpark Pottery. We four children would deliver bread and cakes at weekends to people living nearby and we were all expected to do jobs around the house.

We would go to church every Sunday morning and on the way home we would visit Granny Tucker at Brookador and she would give us a biscuit and a glass of home-made wine. Doll and I were always very well dressed and had a dressmaker in Torquay. My Dad was given the recipe for a fruit cake by Billy Adams' cook; they were called Weston cakes after the name of Billy's house.

The Revd Fagan was a dear old man. When my sister Dorothy was born my mum had a poisoned arm and so he gave her a bottle of wine saying 'I never let my right hand know what my left hand does.' His pet subject for a sermon was 'that little word if,' i.e., if only. Revd Fagan collapsed at the font, having just handed the baby back to its mother, and died. [The *Mid-Devon and Newton Times* of 3 May 1924 reported on the Revd Fagan's demise, noting that he 'had been unable to take duty for three months, since, in fact, he was taken ill during a christening service. His condition, however, was not regarded as critical until last week end, when he was suddenly taken worse, passing away on Sunday, of heart failure.']

Revd Newland-Smith arrived when I was ten and he lived in the big house in Pound Lane which he had built. The Sisters of Mercy from Cary Castle, Torquay, came and lived in the Old Vicarage to help him run the parish as he was High Church. There were about six of them and I remember Sister Margaret the best. They helped run the girls' club in the old Conservative Hall in Water Lane which was originally the Methodist Chapel; it was later to become a workshop for the builder Gordon Norrish. The Sisters of Mercy held Sunday classes and took us on outings; they were very nice. Then came young Revd Dawe who got married to a doctor from Barton and moved into the Old Vicarage and had one daughter. After that came Revd and Mrs Rowe and she ran a school for those aged 4–7 years at the Vicarage.

I went to Kingskerswell School; the teachers I remember were Miss Davis, Mrs Tucker, Mrs Watkins, Mrs Ford and the headmaster was Mr England. When I was seven my parents paid four guineas a term for me to go to Junior Grammar School which was next door to the Clarence Hotel beside Torre station. The house was called Gainsborough and I used to catch the train from Kingskerswell. All us four children went to Senior Grammar School which was next door to South Devon College. The boys were on one side and girls on the other. One of the maths teachers was Arthur Marshall who became famous on the 'Call my bluff' TV show.

My parents paid for our education out of their business; bakers' shops were essential then and there were three in Kingskerswell, baker Moores on the bridge and baker Wyatt at 26 Fore Street and ours, Bovey's, at 3 Fore Street. Don Embury's mother and father started the family butchery at Kerswell Arch and his brother Henry started the first electricity supply in the village at Whitpot Mill. He used the water-wheel and we were one of the first to have electric. This was partly due to the fact that my Gran had left the gas stove on and gassed the parrot Polly that my cousin George Mitchell brought back from Nigeria when he retired from the Army. Everyone was upset, I was 12 and Uncle Bill Gully was home on leave from the Navy so he made cups of coffee and walked me around the garden to help the effects of the gas wear off.

Another butcher was Milverton & Simmons at Brookador farmhouse. He would come and kill our pigs in the shed at the bottom of the garden. Another one was Mr Banbury and his son Frank whose shop was where Bedfords is now. Policeman Brock had two daughters; one was called Bessie. He lived in the police house next to where Sid Gale is now. Then the police house changed to the end terrace at the top of Marguerite Way. Mr Menhennick who built the bungalows in Mount Pleasant Road lived there when

the police station moved to the corner of Broadgate Road. Henry Butt was a porter at Kingskerswell Station and Mr Wyatt was stationmaster. Silas Hill was the blacksmith and he worked opposite the Health Centre with his son William. Holmleigh in Fluder Hill was a big house owned by the Ravenscroft family and they were the last people in the village to have a coach and coachman. The horses were black and Mr and Mrs Nicks (Gertrude) were the gardener and cook.

We had a dog called Kit, she was a brown spaniel, and Charlie Brooks and Silas Hill would borrow her to go shooting rabbits and maybe other things! When Aunt Jess had the Seven Stars Charlie would send Kit from the bakery to the pub and she would go in the pub and find whatever he had touched and bring it back. She was a very clever dog. I remember Farmer Judd from the farm opposite the Barn Owl Inn committing suicide in his shed. His ghost was said to haunt the place. There was also a female ghost at the brewery that became Stentifords Farm. Miss Philpotts lived in Fore Street; she was the sister of Eden Philpotts who wrote books. Next door to her at No.41 lived Major Spence and he would raise the Union flag in his garden on Empire Day. I had a very happy childhood in Kingskerswell and am now the oldest resident that was actually born in the village.

GWEN RICHARDSON'S SCRAPBOOK

The following has been taken from a scrapbook loaned by Mrs Margaret Matthews and recorded by Gwen Richardson in 1982, the Jury family's eldest sister who has since sadly died.

This story about William and Ethel Jury has been written by me, their eldest daughter, as a tribute to them, and particularly for my nephew Kingsley and my niece Gillian. If they or their children feel the urge to explore their past, this is a base on which to start. The two outstanding characters in our family were John Hart and his daughter Ethel who was my mother.

The little we know of Grandmother Hart's family is from our mother's memory of her childhood. She recalled being taken to the South Hams district to visit her aunts. These were her grandfather Michelmore's

Jury's Corner, c.1940.

VILLAGE LIFE RECALLED

Left: *Westhill Terrace and Jury's Corner, 1905.*

Below: *The Jury family, at the turn of the nineteenth century. The parents are seated. Standing left to right are: Edmund, Alfred, Emma (with parents), Elizabeth, Robert, William, Louis Dillon (fiance to Elizabeth). The photograph was taken in front of Westhill House.*

Below: *William Edward Jury standing with Carlo outside his wheelwrighting shop, Westhill House, proud with his newly made cart. Westhill House is now the home of the library at Jury's Corner.*

Right: *The Jury family, c.1900. Emma is standing between her seated parents, William and (Elizabeth) Jane, and, left to right, are: William, Alfred, Elizabeth, Robert and Edmund.*

Below: *John and Emily Hart, c.1885. John is in his bandsman's uniform.*

Below: *Elizabeth and Ethel Hart, with little Beattie Hicks outside 7 Rose Hill, Kingskerswell.*

people and, as mother recalled, farming folk. They are buried in Stokenham churchyard in the South Hams. Her grandfather was by all accounts a dear old man, short and with a beard. Her Grandmother Michelmore is recalled as being something of a virago and she looks a bit fierce in her photograph, but we must remember that they were very poor, had six children and that she spent long hours sewing to help bring the children up. They had one son, Harry, a bachelor, who, threatened with tuberculosis, emigrated to New Zealand, there married his housekeeper and had seven children. His sister Beatrice and her husband went to New Zealand with him.

Three daughters died of tuberculosis, including Sarah and Selina, one of whom left a baby-in-arms who, according to the custom of the time, was taken to the funeral as a mourner. Our Grandmother Emily also died aged about 38 of the same complaint which was the scourge of the age. One daughter Bessie lived to a good old age. She married Samuel Luscombe and they lived in the stone cottage at the bottom of Halls Lane. I remember going with my sister Marion, when we were children, to tea there. There was an orchard, a pony in the old stone outbuildings, chickens and a ferocious terrier dog called Spot who scared the life out of us as he did also, I presume, any venturesome tramp or intruder. I remember how spotlessly clean Great-Aunt Bessie was, the basins turned up on the dresser and the mass of photographs in the front room which seemed to cover every bit of the wall.

Uncle Sam was a cheery little man with a brown wrinkled face. He was known as a champion draughts player, but was once – to his chagrin – beaten by my schoolgirl sister Mavis. Sam and Bessie had two children. Lil, who returned to Kingskerswell in her old age, lived to be nearly 90. Their son Harry was a ne'er do well. He had two daughters, Margery and Dorothy. Margery's children continue to correspond with their New Zealand cousins.

This little anecdote reveals how very strict were the standards of the time. The evening before they were married John and Emily stood at the gate saying goodnight. Her mother looked at the clock and came out. 'It's nine o' clock Emily' she said.

Grandfather John Hart was born at Jetty Marsh, Newton Abbot, in 1860. His father had some sort of job with the Codner Cider people and I believe he used to go to London by stagecoach for them (he died aged 56). Grandmother Hart was a lovely looking woman and our mother remembered her as a loving granny to whom she ran when she was in trouble.

They had several children [including] William, who married Susan and lived in Exeter. They were a tall handsome couple; he very much resembled King Edward VII. I remember my Grandfather telling me that his brother William ran away from school and had little education, but he became a partner in the pottery works of Hart & Moist in Exeter, and brought up his family of seven children in comfortable circumstances.

Grandfather John Hart had three sisters; Polly married Tom Dart and lived in Kingskerswell, she was the mother of our dear Aunt Elsie whom I loved so dearly, and another daughter Lucy was herself the mother of three daughters, one of whom married Erin Brooks. Emily married Charles Pack and lived at Newton. She seems to have been the least well off of the family, but she was well loved. Of their children Emma lived to be over 80 and Alice 92. I visited her on her 90th birthday; she was a charming good-looking woman looking 15 years younger than her age. Their two brothers Bill and Charles joined the police and sadly Jack was drowned as a young man while on holiday in Cornwall.

There was one 'black sheep' in Great-Grandfather's family who would have been less ill thought of in these more liberal-minded days. He married a London girl, 'a flighty bit' by all accounts, who left him and his son and went to London. To be left with a family in those days for a working man was a predicament he solved in the only sensible way. He lived with a common-law wife for the rest of his days. She brought up his son with theirs. When in later years it would have been possible for them lawfully to be married, they didn't bother. This brother George I never saw and only heard about in later years. He lived in Abbotskerswell. I am told that our Grandfather John Hart used to visit him. John and George had another sister Susan who married Bill Knapman and lived in Teignmouth. They had five children,

Of a family of whom I heard little but good, our Grandfather John Hart was a prime example. He was a good, kind and loving man and our mother adored him so much that when I was a child I almost thought he was God. I certainly thought he could do no wrong. He was a gardener to Mrs Hyde at Gara Lodge and married Emily Michelmore who was a maid there. It was Mrs Hyde who gave them the tenancy of No.7 Rose Hill when they were married, and it has been our family home since that time, nearly 100 years. Mrs Hyde thought a great deal of John, whom she recognised [as having] a good brain, and she offered to have him educated, and in later years I think he regretted not availing himself of the offer. He educated himself by reading and the quality of his intelligence and character was recognised by the people for whom he worked, and by whom he was loved and respected.

He was politically aware and became a member of the Labour Party when it was hardly respectable to do so. He was one of the founders of the Working Men's Club in the village. In his early life he played the cornet and was bandmaster of the village band. He was on the Parish Council, a trustee of the Congregational Church and superintendent of the Sunday School.

His life was touched by much sorrow. Emily his wife was always delicate and in her 39th year died of tuberculosis, leaving him with four children – the eldest my mother, who was 16 years old. They had married on Nov. 1st 1884, on her 20th birthday. For the rest of John's life, flowers were always put on her grave on that date.

He had two daughters other than my mother – Ethel Margaret and Emily Sarah (both always known as Meg and Min), but his three sons all died, two in infancy and Ralph on Oct. 25th 1906 in his 19th year. This was a shattering blow to John, whose hair I'm told turned white the night his son died. Some time before Ralph's death John had married again. She was Elizabeth Ham, a dressmaker in the village, a maiden lady, a Sunday School teacher and rather staid. She continued dressmaking after marriage, while Ethel did most of the housework.

I think a little should be written about the Grandma we knew and loved. She was a real mother to Minnie, who scarcely knew her own mother, but it was the birth of the first Grandchild, myself, which completed her standing in the family. She was the only Gran we ever knew, she loved us, gave Marion and I lovely holidays for a month each year and was helpful and generous to our parents. She takes her place in the family records as a well loved member. She died in 1937.

John Hart lived to be 78. He died the May before the World War started in 1939. I came to live with him during the last winter, which is how I came to continue the family connection with Rose Hill.

John and Emily Hart's second daughter, Meg, married Sidney Stephens, who had a butcher's business at Newton Abbot and later at Teignmouth. They had one son, Clifford. Their youngest daughter Minnie married Arthur Pearse in the early years of the First World War [see p63]; Marion and I were two of her bridesmaids. Both Meg and Min died in 1984.

There is a memorial stone to the memory of John and Elizabeth Hart on the walls of Kingskerswell Congregational Church [Now the United Reformed Church].

This tale has come down from an old lady who was a maid at Gara Lodge at the same time as John and Emily. It concerns morning prayers, which were conducted every morning, all staff present. Grandfather, then not much more than a boy, came in from his gardening duties to play the flute, white gloves being donned for the purpose. The repertoire was limited, 'Greenlands Icy Mountains' on one morning, 'Onward Christian Soldiers' the next. Old Mrs Bovey recalled that, with the other young maids, she tried to make him laugh while he played – I wish I had known this story while he was alive and find it difficult to equate my grey-bearded Grandfather with the young whistle-blower.

Our mother Ethel, John Hart's eldest daughter, was born on August 5th 1885. She talked to us a lot about her young days. During her childhood she spent much of her time at Gara Lodge – Mrs Hyde – who died when she was 12 – regarding her it seems as a well loved grandchild, whom she would have adopted

had her parents been willing. That Mrs Hyde was very attached to John and his family is witnessed in the gift of a house she made to him in her lifetime, the double-fronted stone cottage in School Road which he later sold. She also enlarged the kitchen at No.7 and added indoor sanitation as the family grew.

Mother left the village school when she was 12 years old, and her education seems to have been very good; she could write, spell and add up in old age far better than many young people. In her reminiscences she told of Mr Symes, the schoolmaster, who taught his own son to say 'sir' to a beggar, of the Congregational Church which the family regularly attended, and the lay preachers who were given hospitality at Sunday dinner, of the time she fell out with her 'old sweetheart' and the shy young man who later became our father [who] was waiting to ask if he could share her umbrella.

The picture she painted was of Victorian life at its best. There were musical evenings around the piano when mother and her father sang duets, and the romances, not to say flirtations, of the sisters. Although in the years before her marriage mother was mostly occupied at home, she did some domestic work for Mrs Dyer, who lived in the first house in Fore Street, next to the bakery. She used to regale us with stories of Mr Patterson, the son of a High Sheriff of London, who was a paying guest there, and who was by all accounts an alcoholic. Mother held the old gentleman in kindly affection and he for her. She told us the tale of the day he hired a pony and trap for them all to go on an outing and appointed mother to take up the reins. Since she had never driven in her life, it didn't seem a very good idea, nor did it turn out so. At the corner of Fore Street by the Old Vicarage, on a very sharp corner, to the words of Fred Dyer calling, 'Give it more 'scoop' my dear, give it more 'scoop'', Mother didn't give it enough 'scoop', and they all came a cropper.

Mother was 24 years old when she married William Edward Jury at the Parish Church, Kingskerswell, on July 18th 1910. It was a marriage that was to last for 66 years.

Grandfather Jury came to Kingskerswell about 1896 from North Devon and bought Westhill House on the main Newton Abbot–Torquay Road. This spot is now known as Jury's Corner. He had been married some years earlier, to Elizabeth Jane Isaacs, and they already had when they arrived in Kingskerswell a family of six children, Elizabeth, Alfred, William, Emma, Robert and Edmund. I just remember Granny Jury; she died in 1915. Mother has told me she was a gentle, timid little woman. I've often thought of the hardship she must have endured in the old house, without much comfort, working hard, and battling with bronchial asthma, from which she eventually died. There is a revealing little tale which was told about Granny Jury holding a candle to light Grandfather's reading of the newspaper. They sat one each side of the kitchen stove, Granny began to nod,

VILLAGE LIFE RECALLED

Jan Roberts sitting on a log.

Springtime in the garden. Hugh Leslie Roberts and Becky (née Mortimer).

Leslie and Edgar Roberts.

Letterhead of H. Roberts & Sons, timber merchants.

Hugh Leslie Roberts' Home Guard certificate.

In the years when our Country was in mortal danger

HUGH LESLIE ROBERTS,

who served from 2 September 1942 to 31 December 1944. gave generously of his time and powers to make himself ready for her defence by force of arms and with his life if need be.

George R.I.

THE HOME GUARD

and as she did so the candle got lower and lower. 'What's tha up to Jane' cried Grandfather in alarm as the paper was about to be set alight!

About our Grandfather Jury, I find it hard to write. His chief virtue was that he was hard-working, but of that he made a vice, for to his sons he was a slave driver, expecting long hours of hard work for little reward, either in money terms or gratitude. He quarrelled with each of them in turn and at different times. They left home. They were each taught a different trade, my father William being a wheelwright and blacksmith. They had a very good business making carts, etc., and during the First World War built up a timber merchant's business. A wood-splitting engine was installed and one could hear the sound of the saw all over the village. I remember as a child seeing the yard being full of trees ready to be cut up, and I remember also seeing the big horses drawing the long drays with the wood down the hill.

Grandfather's eldest daughter Elizabeth died when she was 20 when there was a typhoid epidemic in the village, in 1901. Alfred, the eldest son, married, went to Devonport during the 1914 war, had one son, also Alfred, and lived until his 80s.

William, our father, also went into the Dockyard at Devonport, as did the youngest son Edmund. He, however, died in the influenza epidemic of 1918, leaving a widow and a young son, George. Alfred remained a bachelor and in later years bought the old home and lived there to a great age. Emma the remaining daughter married Hugh Roberts who looked after the timber side of the business. He in later years took it over to his own property and continued the business there. They had two sons, Edgar and Leslie. Emma died in 1946. Grandfather married again in his late 70s, a maiden lady who died before he did in '93. For some time before his death he lived alone in the big house with only his niece Mabel Heard to care for him. That she was there reveals just one chink in his armour of hardness. She was an orphan, the daughter of his sister Ellen. He took her as a child into his own home and she took her place as another daughter. I like to remember this act of kindness, when I find myself making a judgement of him. I think about the times he lived in and the stock from which he came. As far as I know, they were small tradesmen with very little means indeed, living in small villages in North Devon, rather remote places and by today's standards primitive living. He drove himself as well as everyone else. Uncle Bob told me he would be up at 4.30a.m. at work and he was known to drive a hard bargain as a businessman. When he died he left nearly £4,000, which was a big sum in those days, especially for a man who started with nothing.

Robert, the last remaining member of the family died on August 1981, aged 95. The old home at Jury's Corner where the family came 90 years ago was sold.

Our Dad William Edward Jury was born in 1884 at Northam, North Devon, and was a 12-year-old boy

when the family moved to Kingskerswell. Mother's first memory of him was of a white-faced boy in a dunce's cap. Punished for being late, the punishment should have been his father's for sending him too late on an errand. Although he had a hard upbringing, Dad didn't seem to have had an unhappy boyhood; growing up in the rough and tumble of a large family with a gentle mother and a capable elder sister, Lizzie, who had she lived might have had a leavening effect on their father.

Dad grew into a good-looking young man with almost black hair, he was very thin, but this belied his strength, for he worked hard and long hours as a blacksmith. He never had a sweetheart other than mother and I think his courting was somewhat unromantic, being subject to his father's demands for work. He loved our mother dearly and as long as he lived.

When our Mother and Father were married on July 18th 1910 there were four years to go before the outbreak of war. Kingskerswell was a small village. There were no bungalows at Huxnor, nor at Southey Lane, no building along the main road from Jury's Corner to the farm at Aller. Broadgate was an attractive house at the end of a drive flanked by an avenue of trees. It was at this house that father as a boy earned 2d. on a Saturday morning cleaning boots, chopping wood and making himself generally useful. There were no cars; a little later father went to London and bought the second car to be owned in the village, but with little capital and no help from grandfather who 'didn't hold with these new fangled things that hadn't come to stay', his idea of a starting a taxi business came to nothing. In all his long life he never owned another car, and the opportunity of starting a car business on such an excellent site was lost.

The 'gentry' travelled around the countryside in governess carts, etc., and the ordinary folk who hadn't got a pony and trap (as Uncle Sam and Aunt Bess had) or a bicycle, used shank's pony or more usually the railway. There were good shops in the village, one of the three butchers being Mr Ball, grandfather of Jabez Petherick, whose shop was the present Post Office.

Mother was married in a white dress and hat, but she caused a good deal of hilarity when we were children by adding that her shoes and stockings were black; apparently only 'the gentry' wore all white. Their first home was at the top of the village, in a house that got very little sun. Somebody suggested bottling some, giving their house the name 'Bottle Sunshine' by which it was always known and spoken of in the family. I was born there the following spring in far too much hurry to enter this wicked world. I was the smallest baby the local doctor had ever delivered and it was entirely due to the devoted nursing of my mother that I survived. She had no mother of experience to advise her, no baby clinic and no incubator to take a 2½lb baby in the first early days. When two years later Marion was on the way, Mother took a dislike to 'Bottle Sunshine' and they moved to a tiny cottage in School Road. The back of these cottages then shared with Rose Hill a cobbled yard with flower-beds under the windows. We two little girls played happily and ran into Grandma's at will. The cottage in School Road was lit by oil-lamps and mother bought her oil regularly from a man who called with his van. She often gave him a cup of tea when he called. One day he said 'thank you' to her by presenting her with a box of scented soap. On his next visit after his cup of tea he departed. I was not yet five and very observant, so I trotted out to the van and said 'Please you forgot the soap.' I don't remember what he said, or whether Mother's face was red, but I do remember I had a scolding.

One hot August day when I was five, I was taken ill with what was then known as infantile paralysis (polio) and for nine months lost complete use of my left leg. Again it was mother's devoted nursing which saved me from being lame and restored my strength. With another baby expected it was time for another move to a larger house, to Westhill Terrace, where, on a cold December day, Mavis was born. I remember that winter of 1916. Marion was sent early to school with me. I remember the snow on the ground, the boys forming a chain to help the little ones across the road by the school, and the cans of hot cocoa sent in by a kindly soul living nearby to warm the children. When war broke out Father joined up, but not being called up he later went to Devonport Dockyard as a toolsmith. He was able to get a house to rent in Glendower Road, Plymouth, where mother and the children joined him. The family lived in Plymouth for 12 years. Their youngest daughter Margaret was born there in 1920. Mother has told me that Dad looked back on his Plymouth days as the happiest of his life. He was a family man and loved his children. He rarely drank, rarely smoked, and went very occasionally to a football match. On Saturday nights he would sometimes go into town taking Marion or me with him and stand in the market listening to the stall men shouting their wares. He would buy a bit of leather to 'top' our boots, and some toffee knocked up by a little hammer from a slab on the stall. He was a contented man. He made the toy which gave us and the children around most pleasure, being an old bicycle frame on small wheels with a bar across to rest one's feet. We dragged it up the hill and rode down; it was known as 'Casey's Court' for some reason and was much in demand. He made me, when I was older, a lovely bicycle which he painted and decorated as he had his father's carts. He was a very clever craftsman. Other than electricity there was nothing he couldn't turn his hand to, but he was too meticulous a worker to have ever made a fortune.

Mother of course was the one who bore the burden of the day. Wages were very low in those days, particularly after the war. Dad kept only a shilling or two for himself, but when rent and rates were paid, Mother was left with only £2.5s.0d. to feed and clothe six people, pay for doctor's bills and medicine and my

books when I was at secondary school. How she did it, we shall never know. She gave us the most wholesome food she could afford. She cooked sensibly, but she has told me since that she regretted not being able to give us fruit, which she couldn't afford. Biscuits too were a luxury, two ounces to be bought if one of us was ill.

I remember Mother shedding tears when cream she sent one of us to get, at such a time, was too milky to spread. I remember coming home from school and finding Mother with patterns and a suit of my Auntie's endeavouring to make two garments for the younger ones. She never bought new clothes for herself and rarely for us. I think this was the only way I felt deprived as a child, especially as I got older, but we were always warmly clad and well shod and it did both our parents great credit.

I remember the smell of the kitchen on a wet night when all the family's wet clothes and boots were put around to dry overnight, Dad having travelled six miles on a pushbike or, later on, on a motorbike from work. We were poor, but we always had a house to ourselves and never shared a home. We had none of the entertainment accepted as normal today. Mother recited poetry to us, Marion and I patronised the local free library and were avid readers. We played the piano – Grandma paid for our tuition – Margaret from a small girl played by ear. On Sunday nights we gathered around the piano and sang hymns. There was a time I made a Christmas tree for the younger ones, made of hazel branches and ivy, which I decorated with tinsel and a few foil-covered chocolate novelties, bought with the contents of my very meagre money box. So touched was a friend of the family when he was proudly shown this, that he sent us a box of shiny balls and a little decorated bird which turned into a 'real' tree, on which the door was locked until Christmas Day. We kept those shiny balls for years and they came back to 'Kerswell' with us. Marion and Mavis were not very strong and went for a time to the Open Air School; later Marion went to the Junior Technical Art School where she did very well and became top girl. I, having passed the scholarship exam, went to a secondary school, in those days higher grade education.

Mother was something of a disciplinarian. I remember she once inspected my homework and it did not come up to the standard she expected. She therefore stood over me while I did it again. Both our parents were strict and expected good standards of behaviour, but it was a warm and loving home to which children of our more affluent neighbours loved to come. Dad had to leave the Dockyard at the end of the war and, after a worrying period of unemployment, he worked first at Framfords Car Firm, and then at Tamerton Foliot as a blacksmith and wheelwright. At the end of the 1920s his work became rather precarious and when at the time his father wrote asking him to come back to 'Kerswell' and work for him, in spite of Mother's misgivings, he went.

1929 was a decisive year in our family affairs. Dad's association with his father, as mother had feared, had not lasted and he was working for his brother. During this time he started building a bungalow later named 'Glendower' and Mother and the girls came up to live before it was even finished. I stayed behind for another nine years in my job before returning to 'Kerswell' and 'Rosehill' to live with Grandad John Hart.

Dad was a wonderful old man, he spent hours in his workshops. We all have something in our homes that Dad made for us, and he was ever ready to help his children or neighbours. He had a motorbike, a very old one until replaced with a gift from Uncle Bob, and it was Mother and Dad's joy and delight to go for an outing together, Mother riding pillion. This they did to within a few weeks of their Golden Wedding. Their Golden and Diamond anniversaries were celebrated at 'Rosehill', Mother's old home and from where she was married. Her two bridesmaids were there as were Dad's brother Rob and Mother's old friend from her childhood, our dear Aunt Maud Gill. Just before the Golden Wedding, Mother had been very ill. As we sat down to the anniversary meal, Mother quietly – and unexpectedly – offered up a short prayer in gratitude for the happiness of their marriage and the joy of their family life. The memory is unforgettable. Thinking of Mother it is her unselfishness that I remember most, she never thought of herself. She was loving, kind and much loved. I remember her love of poetry recalled from her schooldays and remarkably repeated to us word perfect when she was over 90. In the frailty of old age she remained the same, grateful for every small care of her. Mother and Dad both lived to be 92 years old, and had 66 years of marriage. We honour their memory, remember them with love and gratitude; may their qualities be seen again in the coming generations.

For all the care you gave us in our childhood,
For going without, that we should have enough,
For sleepless nights with fretful ailing infants,
Being content when things were very tough,
For singing 'rounds' and reading books and poetry,
For keeping me at school when you were poor,
For being at the train on Monday morning
And for 'our home' an ever open door,
There's nothing we could say enough to thank you
And nothing we could do would half repay,
Our very dearly loved and loving mother,
Who celebrates her 90 years today.

Dated August 5th 1975

MRS MARGARET MATTHEWS (NÉE JURY) LOOKS BACK

My Jury family came from the Beaford/Northam area of North Devon and records date back to 1740. Both my sister Mavis and I attended Kingskerswell village school when Mr England was headmaster. He had been gassed in the First World War. The next head-

master after him was Mr Weaver. At age 15 I left school and joined the firm of Williams and Cox in Torquay and worked there as a dressmaker for three years.

When, however, World War II broke out, my sister Mavis and I joined the WRAF, had four weeks training at Morecambe and worked as clerks for the whole of the war. After the war I rejoined for another two years. It was while at primary school that I first met my future husband Leonard Matthews. In 1944 he was in Palestine and we married in 1952 in Kingskerswell Church. Mavis married in Torquay and came to live in Fore Street, Kingskerswell, in a rented cottage paying 50p per week to Mr Wm Adams who collected the rent.

My grandfather, Mr John Hart, played the cornet in the brass band in the village. Len's grandfather Thomas Woollacott also played in the band. The Woollacotts lived before in 'The Gables' in Fore Street, and I remember the brass instruments for the band being stored there.

I remember going to the village school with my sister and coming home to Willake Road every day for lunch. The school bell was rung for return to school and because the village was quiet in those days the bell could be heard throughout the entire village. Mavis and I would run back via Jury's Corner to the school, because we could not cross the fields that existed along the main road at that time.

There was a small school in what was Mr Dennis Flower's house in Fore Street run by a Miss Bellamy, and Gwen our elder sister went there when she was about four in 1915. There was also a small school run by Mrs Rowe, the vicar's wife, in the Old Vicarage in about the 1950s. Also a Miss Wale had a small school in a timber shed at the bottom of her garden as it abuts Southey Lane/Fore Street. I remember also that on Sundays the village was packed with people going to all the churches, sometimes three times a day.

Westhill Terrace, Kingskerswell, has an unusual history. The conveyance for the parcel of land No.361, (Tithe Map No.64), known as 'Lane End', for the proposed Terrace, was dated 3rd August 1898, and was between James Woollacott, Thomas Stookes and others, the purchase price being £132. Westhill Terrace Nos 1–12, were built by James Woollacott, Len's great-grandfather. Starting at the far end, the houses were built crescent shape following the curved outline of the field, thus allowing more space. The first three were built at the turn of the century, and according to the Census of 1901, houses Nos 1 and 2 were occupied by members of the Woollacott family. The 1905 Ordnance Survey map of Kingskerswell shows eight houses on the site, the first four built of stone.

James built the houses to give his employees work during inclement weather when conditions didn't allow for other outside jobs to be done. This was known in the trade as a 'hospital job'. Although the houses were basic, they were considered 'modern' at that time and consisted of three bedrooms, hall, sitting-room, kitchen (with range), wash-house and outside toilet, a large front garden and a backyard. They were let at a weekly rent of 2s.6d. rising to 3s.6d. by 1916. Wages were low, and £1 a week was considered good for a manual worker.

I remember my father, William Jury, telling me that the cost of materials for each house was approximately £64. Much of the materials used had been recycled; nothing was wasted. Jury and Sons, Wheelwrights and Coachbuilders of Westhill House, did much of the work. Discarded materials from other building projects were altered and used again. Because James had six children, when he died in 1913, two houses each were inherited by his surviving children, Nos 11 and 12 by his son Thomas, also a builder.

Adjacent to No.12 was a spare piece of ground sloping down to Coffinswell Lane which was much narrower at that time with hedges and trees lining the route to Coffinswell village. A high stone wall replaced the hedge and the slope [was] filled in, thus making the small plot large enough for a pair of semi-detached houses, Nos 13 and 14, which were erected in 1915. Fifteen steps lead to a path which is a right of way to the front gardens of the Terrace. When Thomas Woollacott died in 1937, he in turn left a house to each of his four children. No.14 is the last to be occupied by the family.

Kingskerswell Funeral 1937: An Account of the Late Mr T. Woollacott

The death took place at Fore Street, Kingskerswell on Saturday 11th December, of Mr Thomas Woollacott aged 69, after a long illness. He carried on business as a builder for many years, but owing to an accident from which he never fully recovered, he had to retire and leave his son to carry on the work. He was a musician of outstanding ability, and acted as Bandmaster to the Kingskerswell Band. He was considered one of the best cornet players in the district, which brought him an offer to join a famous band, which he refused owing to his business. He served on the Parish Council, was gravedigger and bell-ringer, and captain for many years of the Bell-ringers. His father, brother, son and he himself during the period 1911 and 1912 were all ringing in the same peal at the Parish Church.

Deceased was a keen supporter of football and was Hon. Sec. of the Aller Vale Football Club which won the Devon Junior Cup in the season of 1893/94. Six of his fellow team members in that memorable match, Messrs T. Causey, F. Whiteway, S. Bradford, S. Hicks, F. Nix and L. Reddaway were his Bearers. He also assisted by playing in the Athletic Rugby Team at Torquay. In politics he was a Conservative and he had been a member of the National Friendly Society practically all his life. He was a native of Kingskerswell and a keen supporter of the Cricket Club.

'Diamond Wedding' Pair Recall when 'Rush Hour' Meant Cattle on the Roads
(taken from a press cutting, 22 July 1970)

The days when the 'rush hour' on the main Newton Abbot–Torquay road meant a vehicle every 20 minutes and horse-drawn wagons and coaches made their leisurely journeys along this unpaved country lane come readily to mind to Mr and Mrs William Edward Jury, who, at the time of writing, have just celebrated their Diamond Wedding.

At their home at 26 Willake Road, Kingskerswell, they recalled many glimpses of their childhood spent in the village. The population then was less than 1,000 with Fore Street and Yon Street the only two residential roads. 'Although we didn't have any traffic like we do nowadays, the roads used to be terrible on Wednesdays' said Mrs Alice Jury, continuing:

They used to drive the bullocks and sheep along the road from Newton Abbot Market to the slaughter-house at the back of Fore Street. It was impossible to walk along the road and if we wanted to go to Newton Abbot, we used to have to cut through the fields to the old Newton Road. It used to cost 5d. return to Newton Abbot or Torquay on the railway; but most people were hard up and had to walk everywhere.

Mr Jury, whose father's wheelwrighting and coachbuilding firm gave its name to Jury's Corner, remembered on many occasions walking to Bidgood's at Wolborough Street, Newton Abbot, and carrying home rods of iron on his back. The family business at one time was run at Northam in North Devon, where Mr William Jury was born in 1884. After a short stay at Thelbridge, near Tiverton, where Mr Jury paid his 'two coppers' for his schooling, the business moved to Kingskerswell and was established at Westhill House.

Attending the C of E Primary School, he was attracted to a girl in the same class. Miss Alice Hart who lived at 7 Rose Hill also went to the same Sunday School and in July 1910 they were married at St Mary's Church, Kingskerswell. With his brothers Alfred, Robert and Edmund, Mr Jury worked in the family business which traded under the name of W.E. Jury & Son at Westhill House.

One of Mr William Jury's earliest recollections is the relief of Ladysmith during the Boer War:

I remember Jack Burridge from Kingskerswell who was one of those locked in at Ladysmith. He wrote and told his mother that they were so hungry they had to eat their horses and then ate the skins.

Occupying pride of place in the Jurys' home was a greetings telegram from the Queen and scores of cards and

THE BOOK OF KINGSKERSWELL

Right: *T. Woollacott labour costs list and total invoice, November 1936, made out to Mr Brown (pictured on p84).*

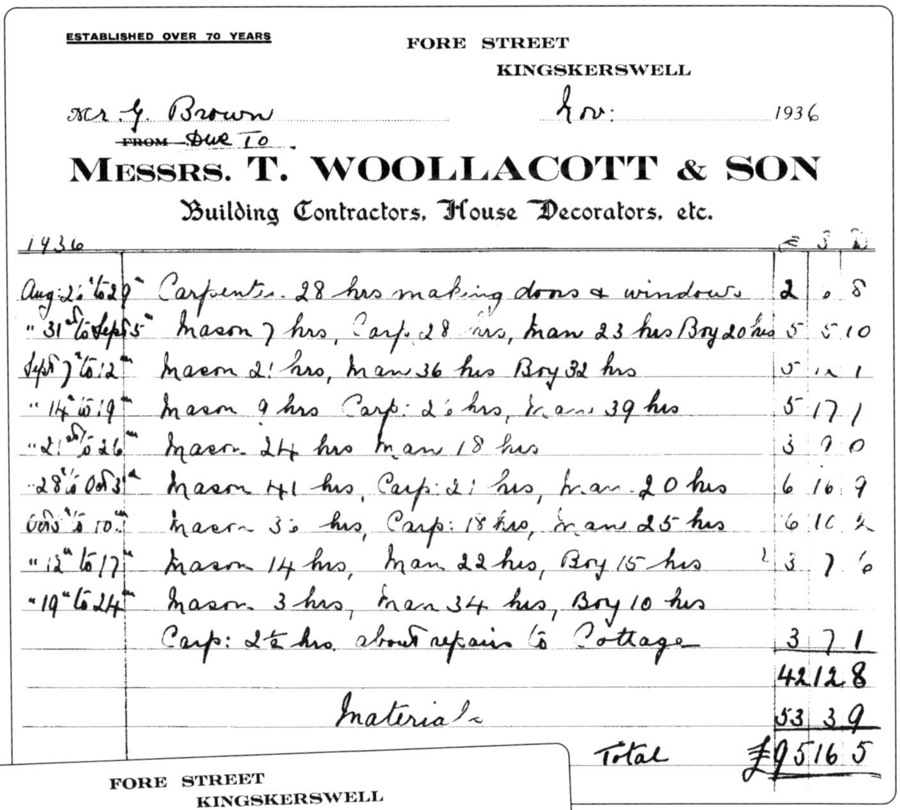

ESTABLISHED OVER 70 YEARS
FORE STREET
KINGSKERSWELL

Mr G. Brown
Nov: 1936

FROM Due To

MESSRS. T. WOOLLACOTT & SON
Building Contractors. House Decorators. etc.

1936		£	s	d
Aug 2 to 29	Carpenter 28 hrs making doors & windows	2	0	8
" 31 to Sep 5	Mason 7 hrs, Carp. 28 hrs, man 23 hrs Boy 20 hrs	5	5	10
Sep 7 to 12	Mason 24 hrs, man 36 hrs Boy 32 hrs	5	1	1
" 14 to 19	Mason 9 hrs Carp: 26 hrs, man 39 hrs	5	17	1
" 21 to 26	Mason 24 hrs man 18 hrs	3	9	0
" 28 to Oct 3	Mason 41 hrs, Carp: 24 hrs, man 20 hrs	6	16	9
Oct 5 to 10	Mason 36 hrs, Carp: 18 hrs, man 25 hrs	6	16	4
" 12 to 17	Mason 14 hrs, man 22 hrs, Boy 15 hrs	3	7	6
" 19 to 24	Mason 3 hrs, man 34 hrs, Boy 10 hrs			
	Carp: 2½ hrs about repairs to Cottage	3	7	1
		42	12	8
	Materials	53	3	9
	Total	£95	16	5

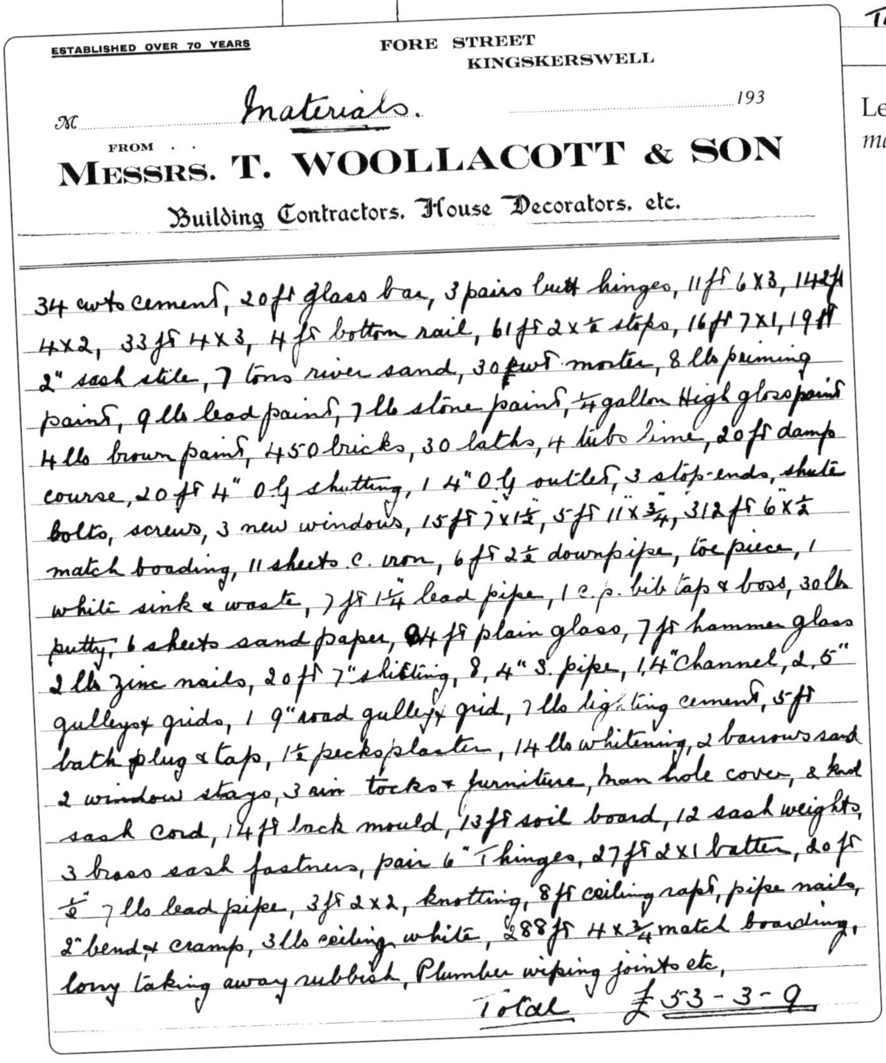

Left: *T. Woollacott materials costs list.*

ESTABLISHED OVER 70 YEARS
FORE STREET
KINGSKERSWELL

M
Materials.
193

FROM

MESSRS. T. WOOLLACOTT & SON
Building Contractors. House Decorators. etc.

34 cwts cement, 20 ft glass bar, 3 pairs butt hinges, 11 ft 6 x 3, 142 ft 4 x 2, 33 ft 4 x 3, 4 ft bottom rail, 61 ft 2 x 1½ steps, 16 ft 7 x 1, 19 ft 2" sash stile, 7 tons river sand, 30 feet mortise, 8 lbs priming paint, 9 lbs lead paint, 7 lb stone paint, ¼ gallon High gloss paint 4 lbs brown paint, 450 bricks, 30 laths, 4 tubs lime, 20 ft damp course, 20 ft 4" O.G shutting, 1 4" O.G outlet, 3 stop-ends, shute bolts, screws, 3 new windows, 15 ft 7 x 1½, 5 ft 11 x ¾, 312 ft 6 x ½ match boarding, 11 sheets C. iron, 6 ft 2½ downpipe, toe piece, 1 white sink & waste, 7 ft 1¼ lead pipe, 1 c. p. bib tap & boss, 30 lbs putty, 6 sheets sand paper, 84 ft plain glass, 7 ft hammer glass 2 lbs zinc nails, 20 ft 7" shilting, 8, 4" S. pipe, 14 "Channel, 2, 6" gulleys & grids, 1 9" road gulley & grid, 7 lbs lighting cement, 5 ft bath plug & tap, 1½ pecks plaster, 14 lbs whitening, 2 barrows sand 2 window stays, 3 air bricks & furniture, man hole cover, 2 bed sash cord, 14 ft lock mould, 13 ft soil board, 12 sash weights, 3 brass sash fasteners, pair 6" T hinges, 27 ft 2 x 1 batten, 20 ft ½, 7 lbs lead pipe, 3 ft 2 x 2, knotting, 8 ft ceiling raps, pipe nails, 2" bend & cramp, 3 lbs ceiling white, 288 ft 4 x ¾ match boarding, lorry taking away rubbish, Plumber wiping joints etc,

Total £53 – 3 – 9

telegrams from well-wishers. To mark the occasion the bells of St Mary's were rung and members of the family and friends attended a party at Mrs Jury's former home at 7 Rose Hill.

JAN HUMPHREY'S CHILDHOOD MEMORIES

You asked about an accumulator, i.e. rechargeable batteries for an old-fashioned radio. Well I do remember them. At my grandfather's house they had a big radio, and every fortnight the accumulator lady arrived to change them. There were two of them in the radio. They were made of glass with coils inside; they had carrying handles and were the shape of a rectangle stood on end. The lady who delivered them always brought her daughter with her. To a child the elder lady seemed about 100 and the younger one was not much younger, but I expect they were quite young. I think they came from Kingsteignton.

Now my grandfather's house was quite old-fashioned; they did not have hot running water or electric lights. There was a gas mantle in the kitchen and hallway, and that was all. If you wanted to go to the toilet, it was down the back stairs and outside. The toilet had a huge wooden seat which was scrubbed every Monday after the washing was done, and no modern toilet paper – it was newspaper hung on a skewer. It was so cold to go down there in the winter. At night you took your candle with you upstairs. If it was winter, also a hot-water bottle, which doubled as your water in the morning to wash with. If you wanted to go to toilet in the middle of the night, you used a pail or pot. Then in the morning you went and emptied it.

Monday morning was always washday. Grandfather (George Mortimore), got up early to get the 'copper' boiling. First he had to fill it from the tap, and light the fire under it, to get it all ready for when my aunt came down to help. It was funny really. This was the 1950s and they still used wash-dollies and mangles, but how white their washing was, blowing on the line. I loved going over there to watch all that happen.

Wednesday was the next interesting day. Grandfather dressed in his best suit and leggings, ready to go to Newton market. We would then go and wait for the Devon General Van to give us a lift into town. Grandfather had the grocery shop where Carter's is now. He would go to town to get paper bags, pay his bills and meet up with his son, who would give us a lift back home again. Dinner was always waiting for us. I often wondered how they knew what time we would be back. It was never the same time but dinner was always ready, just being put on the table.

It was roast lamb, potatoes, veg., and a type of suet pudding, which was tied up in a cloth and boiled. I forgot to mention that all hot water had to be boiled on an old black range. There were three kettles on it all the time. Cold meat was kept in a meat safe, cheese, in a cheese dish. It used to have great big cracks in it as it dried out, but I say this: that cheese had more flavour than today's.

Then they had electricity installed in the late 1950s but still did not have a fridge, washing machine or hoover; everything was done as it had been before. Mondays after the washing was done the water was used to scrub the toilet seat, and the back stairs. The rest was used to scrub the backyard. I can remember the backyard crumbling in, there was a disused well there that no one knew about, so it had to be capped and made safe. I can remember my mother telling the story of how Grandma would have the windows facing the road wide open, and a traction engine would go by, and the sparks used to come in the windows and singe the net curtains.

Now, this gas mantle in the kitchen; it had a life of its own. One minute it would be burning brightly, then it would 'pop' and go down so dim you could hardly see. Then it would 'pop' and come back bright again. The one in the hall only seemed to be lit at Christmas and special occasions.

As there were no other lights in the house, you would use a candle, to either go down to the toilet, or up the stairs to bed. It sounds quite simple, light the candle, and off you go. In theory it should have been, but you had to take into consideration the down draught in the bend of the stairs. An old aunt that also lived there was forever singeing her hair. In the winter it was nothing for their false teeth to freeze in the glass. You can see why I have a funny sense of humour.

As grandfather got older and had problems doing his gardening, a chap used to come and help. He would spend the morning planting cabbages, come and say bye, then grandfather would go down to see what kind of job he had made of it. It was never right. So grandfather would hand-over-hand go down his stick, pull out the cabbage plant, move it half an inch or less and replant it and come back up the stick hand-over-hand, and move on to the next plant, until in the end he had replanted the whole lot.

There was a big apple orchard, grandfather kept chickens and geese there, at the bottom of the orchard. Wilf Huggins kept his horse in the field out over the hedge from Grandfather's orchard. That field is now part of Manor Road. Wilf Huggins used to go around the village selling fruit and veg. from his horse and cart. Wilf also had a shed up behind the old Seven Stars public house, where he kept the fruit and veg. The old public toilets sort of ran along beside the back of the Seven Stars.

Getting back to my grandfather's, next door, he had a flat (which is now the pink painted place) which he rented to his sister-in-law. Underneath, it was a trap house and a stable next door for your horse. It always had a smell of its own. There had not been horses there for years.

Also there was a bakery; it was known by the family as the 'bakehouse' complete with bread ovens, but as Grandfather had signed a form to say he would not start up a bakery, it was never used. As children he would take us grandchildren and weigh us, measure us and write it on the wall of the bakehouse. So when the place was sold it would have had all our names, weights and heights written on the wall.

In the 1960s a big event took place over there; grandfather had a toilet put indoors upstairs (but still no hot running water) and a TV. Before this the only thing to amuse you was the radio or an old gramophone. It was quite a grand looking thing, with a big brass trumpet, or you could play cards, but not on a Sunday. You could do needlework if the light was right, or knit. This was easier as you didn't need to follow the pattern very much. BUT never on a Sunday. The only thing you could do on Sundays was go to church and go for a walk. Reading this now people would never believe how old-fashioned it all was and how things happened over there.

Grandfather sold paraffin in the shop. If someone wanted some, I can remember going down the garden to the 'oil house' to get it for him. The News of the World *advertised their paper on a board attached to one of his walls and paid him a shilling a year for doing it.*

My grandfather was a very easy-going grandpa to us grandchildren, he would give us anything. He died in 1970. The aunt who lived with him moved into the flat with her sister (she had been Grandma's sister, Grandfather's sister-in-law, Aunt Barrie Truscott). There it was just as old fashioned – no bathroom, just a toilet, no proper kitchen, but this aunt who lived there first did have a fridge and a TV. The only door to the outside was the one that opened on to the main road. To get her washing down to the garden she put it into a basket and lowered it down on a piece of rope; when it was dry, it came up the same way. Even the cat went up and down the same way. The little flat had two bedrooms, a toilet, kitchen and a living-room. It was not very warm as the stables and trap house were right under it and they were very draughty; there was not a lot of insulation between the two.

When you think the council-houses at this time had bathrooms, hot water and all mod-cons, my grandfather was living in the past, well and truly. Just going back for a minute, I forgot to say the only heating at Grandfather's was the old black range in the kitchen. Once you left the kitchen it was freezing cold. You only went into the 'parlour' at Christmas. This was the only two days that the fire got lit in there. If you went in there any other time of the year, it would have to be for something special, or to play the piano. I think the right term would be 'A Victorian household'.

WINIFRED FARLEY REMEMBERS

My maiden name is Winifred Doris Honeywill and I was born in 1912 in 9 School Road, Kingskerswell, on Christmas Eve. My younger brother Donald was born two years later in 1914.

Our father spent most of his working life at Stoneycombe Quarry and our mother and grandmother had a laundry in the village. Clothes were collected from the big houses in the village, and our mother took over the starching and pressing of fine linen and lace. The laundry was then delivered back to the houses by all three of them. The laundry was situated at the bottom of Daccabridge Road in what became 'Davies & Miller'.

Above: *Louise and Samuel John Honeywill, with their children Donald and Winifred, c.1924.*

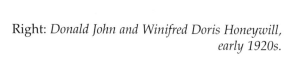

Right: *Donald John and Winifred Doris Honeywill, early 1920s.*

VILLAGE LIFE RECALLED

Ron and Win Farley, 1953, at their wedding at the Methodist Church.

Mrs Win Farley, née Honeywill.

Stoneycombe (now demolished), Bickley Road.

My first experience of going to school was at the age of three and I was brought home again. I used to watch the schoolchildren going past our house to the village school and remember thinking how nice it would be to go as well. However, my wishes were realised as I did eventually go to the village school about a year or two later. The headmaster at that time was Mr England. We did a great deal of sewing, which was taught to the girls at that time by, I think, a Miss Guy. The dentist used to visit the school on a regular basis.

At age 11, I caught the train into Newton Abbot to Wolborough Road School. But when I was 13 I became almost totally blind and had to give up my schooling. My routine changed radically as instead I regularly had to go to Exeter General Hospital on the train for treatment to my eyes and I eventually regained my sight. After that I then became a domestic in Kingskerswell and, when my mother became ill, I looked after her.

When I was a young girl I remember the farm across the road from our home in School Road. It was called Rose Hill Farm and had a large orchard with many apple trees. The Health Centre is now standing on this site. Mr Foss senr, Peter's father, ran the farm.

Mr Crocker taught me along with many others to dance around the Maypole. The teaching was carried out on Kingskerswell Downs. I also remember the beating of the bounds in 1923 and recall walking it with my brother Donald, and I can be seen in pictures of this occasion and can be picked out easily.

When the Second World War started, I worked in a factory in Kingskerswell called Tecalemit which made pipes for carrying water. It was situated on the Coventry Farm site near the Halfway House Inn (and was later called Gabriel Engineering).

I was a regular Wesleyan Church member and met my future husband, Ron Farley, when he came to Kingskerswell to preach. We married in 1953 and then moved to our present address in Newton Abbot. However, I continued to catch the bus and work in the factory in Kingskerswell. Ron was a postman in Newton Abbot.

Fred Crocker and Kit Warman in School Road, Kingskerswell.

I have had a happy life. My mother, father and brother were all close and I have had a happy marriage. When a child, we never took holidays as such, but would occasionally go to Plymouth or Exeter on the train for the day. Another favourite outing of ours was to go by train or bus to Dartmouth and out on the River Dart, then at the end of the day cross over on the small ferry to Kingswear to catch the train home again.

ANNETTE EVERETT'S RECOLLECTIONS

I came to Kingskerswell in 1966 with my then husband Nigel and two boys Daniel, then five years old, and Dominic, aged two. We moved into 'Southernhay', 1 Southey Lane. I can just remember that the new bridge was being built over the main road at the time of the purchase of Southernhay. We bought the property for £5,750 from a Miss Newton who was bedridden and lived in the downstairs living-room. She was cared for by Miss Bond who had a house in Brookador.

The house was a very beautiful, large listed late-Georgian house with an irregular-shaped garden. Part of it, I later discovered, was much older, the then kitchen probably dating from about 1600 or so. We found when we climbed into the roof of this part that the old thatch was still intact underneath the existing slates. The deeds showed that this building and the land were sold by the St Marychurch and Keyberry Turnpike Trust in about 1835.

At about that time Mr Stooke, a timber merchant, built the main house called Southernhay. The land opposite in Southey Lane became his timber yard. As a result of his occupation all the doors in Southernhay were very solid and of good timber. There were two large doors about ten foot or so high connecting the two main living-rooms on the ground floor. I later had all the doors stripped and they were a beautiful honey-coloured pine. The walls had been painted dark red and I presume that this was the original decoration. The ceilings were finely moulded and the downstairs also consisted of a toilet, a utility room with old-fashioned ceiling clothes dryer, a dining-room and a large kitchen, with several large walk-in cupboards leading off.

On the first floor which was reached by a beautiful mahogany staircase were three double bedrooms, a bathroom and separate toilet. On the second floor were a further three large rooms, one with a small ornate Victorian cast-iron grate. I must mention that there were also on the ground floor three marble mantelshelves and grates, one of Ashburton marble and another of Petitor marble. There was a large cobbled cellar. Interestingly, the cellar, I later learned, had been earmarked by the Civil Defence for their exclusive use in the event of 'enemy action'.

In the backyard was a 40ft-deep well. I later exposed all the cobbles in this yard which were hiding underneath two or three inches of concrete. The front garden was in the form of a triangle and had a very old pear tree, nectarines, apple trees and a fig tree. This odd-shaped piece of garden is possibly explained when one looks at the 1838 Tithe Map, as illustrated, from which it appears to have originally been a corner part of a larger field. On the Tithe Map, fields 316, with the house, and 317, across the road in Southey Lane, must have been a single piece through which the Turnpike Trust created or diverted the link with Fore Street. The adjacent fields to the east, with 'Townsend' in their name, may well reflect an older limit of the village at this junction.

The village had many shops and since this was prior to the days of the supermarket, I think many people used their local shops. There were two bakers, a chemist, the Co-op, Dorothy Unwin, a grocer, and two butcher's shops – Banbury and Embury, Mrs Sagar's ironmongers, a vegetable shop run by Mr Fraser (assisted by Mrs Gale) and a further grocer's called Codds where the car park in Fore Street now stands, not forgetting the Post Office, three hair-dressers and a shoe-repair shop. In Yon Street was Wildig's Stores. On the main road was Mr Gibson another grocer, a paper shop Daymans and the chemist's shop which has now moved up into Fore Street. There was also another hairdresser which is still there.

My eldest son was attending a private school in Newton Abbot at the time of the house move but later with my younger son attended the village primary school. The head teacher at the time was Mr Powell. This school was in the building which is now the home of the Community and Leisure Centre.

Mr and Mrs Brown, 36 Southey Lane.

VILLAGE LIFE RECALLED

Southernhay, Fore Street, with the Fluder junction, 1996.

Right: *Tithe map extract showing Southey Lane link through field 316/317, to Fluder Hill/Fore Street, created by the Turnpike Trust in the early-nineteenth century.*

The same view during the 1960s.

Left: *Kingskerswell School, c.1910.*

Right: *Kingskerswell School, c.1920s.*

Left: *Kingskerswell Community and Leisure Centre, Dobbin Arch, September 2000.*

Chapter 7
WHEN WE WERE SO VERY YOUNG
A Photographic Portrait

Left: *Kingskerswell School's 1950s costume play. Left to right, back row: Peter Martin, David Bond, Kenny Nicks, Robin Brown; middle: Cherilene Cheesman, ? Jeffrey, Peter Hutton, Alan Martin, Sylvia Avery, Nancy Underhill; front: June ?.*

Right: *Kingskerswell School's 1950s costume play. Left to right, back row: Freddie Dodd, David Bratcher, Roger Moon, Joy Hutton, Nancy Underhill, ?, ?, ?; front: Edward Stentiford, Kenny Nicks, Sheena Brown, ? Hern, Fiona Sheffield, Brenda Stuckey, Linda Evemy, ?.*

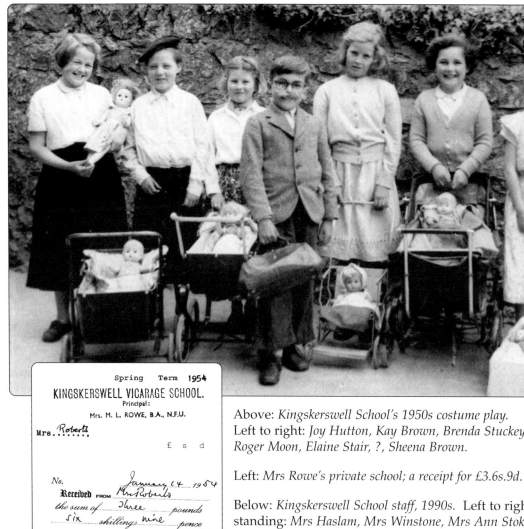

Above: *Kingskerswell School's 1950s costume play. Left to right: Joy Hutton, Kay Brown, Brenda Stuckey, Roger Moon, Elaine Stair, ?, Sheena Brown.*

Left: *Mrs Rowe's private school; a receipt for £3.6s.9d.*

Below: *Kingskerswell School staff, 1990s. Left to right, standing: Mrs Haslam, Mrs Winstone, Mrs Ann Stokes, Mrs Gwen Palmer, Mr Grahame Rowell, Mrs Ann Pilling, Jane Atkins, Miss Tutton (Mrs Wolf); seated: Mrs Sheen, Mr Bob Hayley, Mrs Powell, Mr Powell, Mrs Kathleen Ridley, Mr Malcolm Upham, Mrs Gill Thorne.*

WHEN WE WERE SO VERY YOUNG

Kingskerswell School, 1928. Left to right, back row: Bill Owen, Lewis Triggs, Victor Aggett, Frank Gale, Henry Hall, Len Matthews, Harold Dart; third row: Freda Dart, Sybil Garrett, Joan Searle, Evelyn Wonacott, Winnie Brown, Grace Dart, Betty Jennings, Peggy Andrews; second row: Wilfred Richards, Arthur Nicks, Evelyn Knapman, Mary Gully, Clara Butt, Marjorie Mitchell, Marie Mortimer, Albert Williams, Stanley Richards; front: ?, Cyril Sampson, Clarence Wilkinson, Roland Elliott, Ronald Channing, Kevin Dogger, Morris Kernick, Roland Hearne.

Kingskerswell School, 1932. Left to right, back row: Frank Gale, Jack Terrell, Peggy Andrews, Grace Dart, Joan Searle, Bessie Stentiford, Peggy Osborne, Evelyn Wonacott, Winnie Brown, Leonard Matthews, Wilfred Howard; middle: Lewis Triggs, Wilfred Richards, Henry Hall, Ronald Channing, Myrtle Gater, Marjorie Mitchell, Betty Walling, Peggy Smale, Betty Jennings, Harold Dart, Victor Aggett, Leonard Uren, Richard Evans, Mr R.W. Weaver; front: Bill Owen, Cosmo Hill, Norman Howard, Eddie Crocker, Clarence Wilkinson, Stanley Richards, Dennis Murphy, Charlie Brooking, Morris Kernick, Arthur Nicks.

Kingskerswell School, c.1890s.

Kingskerswell School, c.1900.

WHEN WE WERE SO VERY YOUNG

Right: *Kingskerswell School 'Band', c.1918. Left to right, standing: Bert Goodman – bugle, ? Cole – flute, Tom Bulley – castanets; seated: Fred Crocker – bass drum ('Kingskerswell Band' on side), Fred Knapman – tambourine, ? Nicks – frying panjo, Tom Wills – little drum, Sam Whiteway – dustbin lid bass.*

Below: *Kingskerswell School Pageant, 15 June 1921.*

Kingskerswell School, early 1900s, 'crossing the line'.

Kingskerswell School, early 1900s, 'a diorama'.

Chapter 8

Aspects of Farming

South Whilborough Farm

This was a medieval landholding on which the present seventeenth-century thatched farmhouse was built, now listed Grade II. A pair of thatched cottages was added before 1838 to house families of farm workers. In 1937 Frederick Wakeham became tenant after the Bowditch brothers and moved from Newton Farm near Blackawton with his wife Ruby and their children Edgar, Rhoda, Gladys, and young twins Eric and Irene. The farm belonged to Mr Ley of Exeter until the Wakeham family bought it in 1963. It was a mixed farm of some 131.84 acres with a hand-milked dairy herd, sheep, pigs and work-horses. There was also a pond with ducks, as well as geese and hens. Apples from the orchards were used for cider for home use.

One full-time and one-part time worker lived in the cottages and there was a worker who lived in the farmhouse. About a quarter of the farm area was cultivated ground. Crops grown, mainly hay, mangolds and turnips, were mostly for animal feed, although oats, wheat and barley were also grown. Contractors worked the side-fields of the valley which were too steep for horse-drawn machinery.

The Second World War brought farming into focus with all farm workers being exempt from military service as they were providing vital supplies. Farm production was government-directed. The concern for home farm production continued after the war but methods began to be modernised: pumped water was replaced with a mains supply, and mechanised milking and tractors reduced the need for hand workers and horses.

Left: *South Whilborough Farm, c.1948. Edgar Wakeham is ploughing the field.*

Right: *South Whilborough Farm; the view over the farm and Kingskerswell village, c.1970*

Right: *South Whilborough Farm, 1930s, with Fred Wakeham and his son Edgar raking hay.*

Left: *South Whilborough Farm, 1940s, with Fred Wakeham and Violet.*

South Whilborough Farm, with Edgar in the yard, 1940.

ASPECTS OF FARMING

South Whilborough Farm, 28 March 1937.

Sheep in Kennel Orchard at South Whilborough Farm.

Red Devon cattle in 'Alderney' at South Whilborough Farm.

Growing family members increasingly married and left the homestead. Gladys married Harry Trant in 1945, Irene wed Herbert Vallance in 1954, finally Eric married Margaret at Denbury, and it was to there that they moved, in 1963. In that same year Frederick bought the farm outright and willed it to his two sons. Edgar remained single, so when his father died in 1967 aged 76 he ran the farm, helped by Eric from Denbury and Mr Sleep in the farm cottage, and cared for by Rhoda who stayed to run the farmhouse.

Egg collecting was done by whoever had the time. Mechanisation meant that work previously done by six workers could now be achieved by one or two, but the pattern of living had also changed drastically. Instead of the crowded bustle of horses and hand workers came the lonely isolation of many hours of machines being used intensively to keep up production, a way of life relieved only by market days and club events.

Particular features of the farm included three known limekilns – one a listed structure, a second all but destroyed in the field called Alderney. The third, deemed too near the farm gate for the safety of children, had been filled in years earlier. The cottage adjoining the plot of ground called Kennel Orchard has an underground store where hounds were kept for the Hunt which used to be run from there. This orchard has a good stone wall around it. The farm horses were shod by Mr Silas Hill and his brother, the blacksmiths who had their forge opposite the site of the Health Centre. Stock was transported by Mr Gill of Chudleigh. A Mr Hall came in to do the combining and threshing. The hay was then brought in and the ricks were thatched, a task completed with the help of outside labour.

By 1990, the year Edgar died, links with Europe led to increased government controls over all aspects of farming. Despite this Eric continued to run the business, travelling daily from Denbury, while Rhoda still ran the farmhouse, but seven years later, on his reaching a pensionable age, Eric decided to retire and so put the farm up for auction. The dispersal sale was well attended, but it was a sad occasion for the

Baling hay at South Whilborough Farm.
Left to right: *Percy and Maurice Sleep (twins), Harry Trant, Herbert Vallance, and Edgar and Eric Wakeham.*

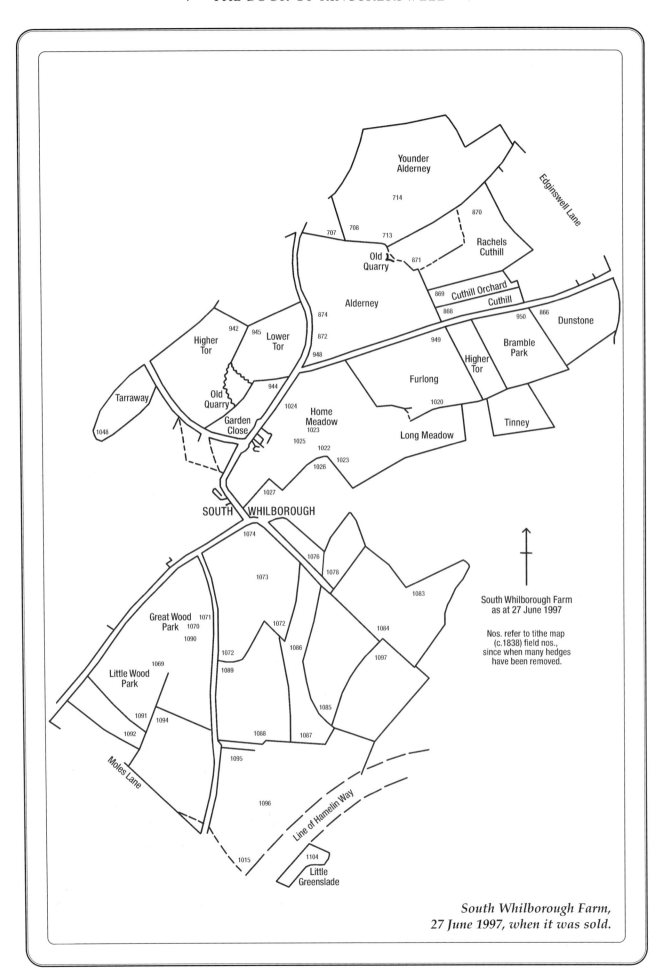

South Whilborough Farm, 27 June 1997, when it was sold.

ASPECTS OF FARMING

South Whilborough Farm.

South Whilborough Farm and South Whilborough Cottages, 1996.

farming community to see yet another farm being lost to private occupation. Now the farmhouse, though looking much the same externally, has a modernised interior and the farm buildings are being adapted for other uses.

One cannot help but wonder how, should future events cause home farming to become essential to our survival once again, the wholesale loss of experience and expertise could possibly be reversed to any good effect. In 60 years this farm has moved through every stage of development to dispersal, a not uncommon illustration of the country's farming history.

LONGLANDS FARM

Set high near the head of, and overlooking, a long valley with attractive views of Kerswell Down and distant views of Kingskerswell, Longlands Farm is one of the few working farms in the area. It was built in about 1930 by the Wale family who had owned many of the fields since 1855. More fields were bought between 1872 and 1925, including one called Longlands on which the farmhouse was built and after which it was named. Other fields include Kneller Orchard, Kneller Field, Lower Kneller Orchard, Lower Meadow, Mouse Hill, Mousehill Meadow, Ray, Stanthill, Yannon and Yeothorn.

In 1956 Mr S.C. Tibbetts bought Longlands from Mr William Wale after previously farming near Bromsgrove in Worcestershire and near Cleobury Mortimer in Shropshire. More recently his son John Tibbetts inherited the farm, and he operates it, together with his wife Eileen, from the bungalow opposite the original farmhouse.

Basically a dairy farm, yet more fields were added during the Tibbetts' occupation and the whole worked well for many years. Sadly, in the wake of the epidemic of foot and mouth in 2001, the control of animal registration and movement became much more rigorously detailed and time consuming. Such strict controls are particularly onerous for a farm with public roads separating its fields and these burdens on Longlands so limited the smooth transfer of cattle between fields and milking parlour that, combined with a suppression of prices for milk yields, milk production has ended. However, the farm has managed to keep animal production viable in an era when Central Government and European policies and controls have stifled most aspects of farming, especially in the South West.

Left: *Traffic hold-up, while sheep arrive at the slaughterhouse behind the old Seven Stars.*

Right: *Rush hour along old Newton Road. Dobbin Arch is on the left and Whitpot Mill leat is to the right, c.1910.*

THE BOOK OF KINGSKERSWELL

Rose Hill Farm

Rose Hill Farm as seen from Fore Street, 1950s.

Left: *The Health Centre on the site of Rose Hill Farm, 1996.*

Rose Hill Farm, early 1900s.

ASPECTS OF FARMING
Coldstray Farm

Mr and Mrs George Webber haymaking at Coldstray Farm in the 1950s. Note the train waiting in the station.

Mr and Mrs George Webber haymaking at Coldstray Farm in the 1950s.

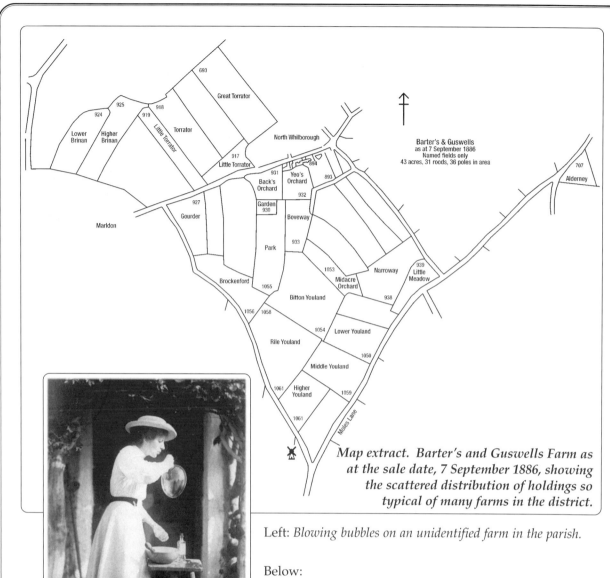

Map extract. Barter's and Guswells Farm as at the sale date, 7 September 1886, showing the scattered distribution of holdings so typical of many farms in the district.

Left: *Blowing bubbles on an unidentified farm in the parish.*

Below:
Foredown Farm, anciently the site of the manor barton of the Manor of Kerswell.

The orchard where Sunnyside Road is today, May 1914.

ASPECTS OF FARMING

Waterdale Farm

Right: *Waterdale Farm with no thatch and dereliction setting in, 1996.*

Below: *Waterdale Farm, partly obscured by a parked vehicle, still thatched, c.1930s.*

Below: *Waterdale Farm – the thatched building in the centre of the photograph, nearest the horse carriage. Note the wall with the milestone on the right-hand side of the 'main' road. The photograph was taken c.1910 before the construction of the Methodist Church.*

Left: *Mrs Stentiford and poultry at Crockwell Farm, 1900.*

Below: *Crockwell Farm, late 1920s. Edwin John Stentiford looks on while horses are prepared for the day's work.*

Below: *'Warick', second-prize winner, July 1923, Newton Abbot. Edwin John Stentiford with stick on the left, and diminutive Silas Hill with his hand on the cart.*

Chapter 9

THE WAR YEARS

MRS JOY GARNER (NÉE HOWARD) RECALLS LIFE DURING THE WAR YEARS

My father, Stanley Howard, and his brothers and sisters also, went to the Church of England school from 1911 onwards. During the war years, 1939–1945, the evacuees came to Kingskerswell and were billeted with local families. We had three girls, two sisters and a cousin. I remember when they arrived... We had gone to bed and my mother called up 'you'd better come down and meet the girls,' which we did. Eventually the cousin went to live elsewhere, but even though we had the two girls for some time, I can't even remember what they were called.

Because we lived in Westhill Terrace it meant crossing the 'busy' main road and Lilian Tozer used to take us, my sister Pam and I, to and from school. The classrooms were very crowded with the extra children. I remember a Mr Webber and a Mr Butcher were teachers. Mr Weaver was the headmaster, Miss Shilston, Miss Bird and Miss Davis were the other teachers; everyone was 'Miss' to us in those days! On the way to school we used to buy a penny Chelsea Bun at Bovey's cake shop just past the War Memorial. We had our gas masks with us every day. On the way, at the top of School Road, was the smithy (blacksmith), and Peter Foss' horses were often in there getting shod. The smell of the burning hooves was awful, the fire glowing and the bellows going, it was quite a frightening place. Opposite of course, was Peter Foss' farm, with lots of orchards fronting on to Hall's Lane. It adjoined the orchard of the Selways.

The school had two air-raid shelters in the playground opposite and we did have to file out and go to them several times. The toilets were outside, and the schoolrooms, for heating, had big black round iron casings for the fire and a black chimney went upwards. Before leaving every afternoon, we had spellings – if you spelt it right, you could go home!

Miss Davis was in charge of the very young children, Miss Shilston taught us to sew and embroider. Mr Weaver taught us all to sing! He was the choirmaster at St Mary's Church, and a lot of the boys were in the choir. We also attended church services when it was Empire Day, or such like, and we all walked over Dobbin Arch and back again. We sat for examinations to go to Newton Abbot Grammar School and South Devon Technical College (just built in the 1940s), Torquay, and many pupils went on to other schools at 11 and 13 years old.

On looking back it was a good school, lots of discipline; we could all write and knew our sums to 12 times table. These were said as a class, altogether, and we certainly learnt them. We also had painting classes and the boys had some football I suppose but I can't remember where as the shelters were in the playground.

We had our meals, midday, at the Constitutional Hall; yes, rhubarb crumble was lovely, and so was stew, and currant pudding. Despite the war I don't think we were hungry. Food was hard to come by. My Dad had an allotment in Coffinswell Lane like a lot of other men and grew much veg. and fruit bushes, gooseberries, blackcurrants, etc. In season we went picking blackberries and got a few apples from somebody. Mr Tozer in Princess Road had ferrets and he caught rabbits. We all went mushrooming and every little helped. Clothes were a problem with the rationing. When my father was young, say, in about 1916, he and his father would catch moles, they were sold when they were skinned.

There were a lot of activities for people to join. You could join the Brownies, Girl Guides, Cubs, Scouts, St John Ambulance Brigade, King's Messengers (a religious club run by a Miss Whiting), Tennis and Badminton Club, Kingskerswell Garden and Allotment Society, Kingskerswell Choral Society, Kingskerswell Drama Group, Cricket Club (which played in the field next to the Park Inn), greyhound racing, dancing at the Public Hall and the Constitutional Hall, and a Youth Club here as well.

Every year a carnival was held, in which everyone took part. There was maypole dancing by the schoolchildren, plenty of ice-cream, and this was held in a field near the greyhound track. Can't remember a band playing...

During the war, the first real black men we saw were American soldiers. They were billeted on Milber Downs, and one Christmas they gave a concert in Coffinswell Church. We kids all walked up Coffinswell Lane in the dark, I shall never forget it.

We, from Westhill Terrace and Princess Road, used to buy our sweet ration at Miss Heard's shop at Jury's Corner. She would crack a sweet in half rather than let you have more than your share! We would watch the American lorries go by and the Americans would throw us Horlicks tablets and chewing gum. Farmer

Peter Foss had fields in Daccombe Lane, and when the cows had to be returned to the farm for milking, they all walked down the Main Street. In those days they all had horns and you would stand back in the shop doorways until they had gone by, leaving the road in a filthy mess, but no one seemed put out by this!

The Girl Guides met in the Parish Rooms in Daccabridge Road. I was a Girl Guide in the Daffodil Patrol. We had to learn our badges, then you could sew them up on your sleeve! It was fun, we learnt such a lot; cooking, sewing, how to light a fire, and do knots, etc. We used to go up on the Downs, light a fire and cook dampers. This was flour and water made into a dough and wrapped around the top of a stick and held over the fire till cooked and blackened! You would take them off and fill them with jam and eat them, soot and all! We also put potatoes in the fire and boiled water in a billy-can for cocoa. That was really fun. We also did stalking on the Downs. You got branches which you used to conceal yourselves as you crawled along on your knees. You moved when the person 'out front' turned her back and she had to guess who you were! We also learnt the Morse Code and did flag signalling from Dobbin Arch to Station Arch. And every so often we went to camp! We joined with other Guides in our Newton Abbot area, from as far away as North Bovey – I still have a lifelong friend from North Bovey from when we all met up at camp at Torpoint. We also went to Staverton where it rained so hard one night (we were in Bell tents), that we all had to sleep in a barn in the hay, above the cattle! Our group was run by Betty Bindloss and Eileen Locke. Betty Bindloss went on to higher things, becoming a Girl Guide Commissioner. Eileen Locke still lives in the village.

The Girl Guides did their bit for the war effort. We used to go to Aller Woods, with sacks, and pick foxglove leaves and some other herb. These were taken to the Invertere Factory (where Moor Park Estate is now), and we, the Guide Company, got paid for it. Eileen Locke from Yon Street was the Lieutenant of the Group and remembers the Baden Powell anniversary. I remember Mr Bouteil used to come and drill the Girl Guides for marching, we even learnt how to slow march.

Many of the children who lived in Westhill Terrace and Princess Road went to the Congregational Church. Mrs Burns who played the organ lived in Westhill Terrace, so it was convenient to all go there together. Every year we had the anniversary at Easter. This entailed having a new dress made and I remember once having straw hats. Mrs Burns used to get leaflets with the music inside and we would go to her house to practice before the big day. Mrs Burns had a rocking chair, and whoever got there first got to sit in the chair waiting for the others. All the Mums and Dads went to the anniversary service (usually in the afternoon), and in our different groups we'd stand out front and 'do our bit'. Mr Edwards was the superintendant. Afterwards we usually ended up walking up around Huxnor and Edginswell Lane and home to Kingskerswell that way.

The greyhound racing track was run by the Bright brothers. Arnold Bright still lives in the Teignbridge area. Many local people were involved, dog walking and parading.

In my day, Mr Saunders was our policeman. He was succeeded by Mr Beer. Both had bikes. The police house was the first house past Broadgate Road, towards the lights.

Stoneycombe Quarry was first a subsidiary of F.J. Moore, Ltd., Plymouth, and supplied lime. Three girls were taxied up from Plymouth every day to run the office! Many local men worked there and walked there every day, even from Coffinswell. Eileen Locke, still living, was one of the three original girls.

Many men from Kingskerswell worked for the Great Western Railway at Newton Abbot. They would ride a bicycle with a carbide lamp there and back, all weathers. When the war was on, many tales were told of 'Double Home' journeys where they witnessed the Blitz in Bristol and London. People from Kingskerswell could see the sky lit up when Plymouth was blitzed.

Armistice Day – there was a parade from Fluder Hill to the Parish Church in the morning. It was pretty impressive and included the Home Guard, the ARP, the St John Ambulance Brigade and, carrying flags, the Brownies, Guides, Cubs and Scouts.

British Legion Sports, 1950. Les Cheesman, cup winner. The presentation was made by Mrs Brown. Mr Jim Taylor, Les' trainer, looks on.

THE WAR YEARS

LES CHEESMAN & FAMILY: SCHOOLBOY MEMORIES OF KINGSKERSWELL 1933–1945

Les and Aubrey Cheesman were born at Forge Cottage in Fore Street in 1933, twin sons of Gladys and Archie Cheesman, and grandsons of Lucy and Albert Goodman who lived next door at 29 Fore Street. Our father Archie was serving with the RAF in Malta at this time. Our sister Wendy was born in 1938 and sister Cherilene born in 1946/47.

We went to Kingskerswell Primary School in 1938/39. The teachers were the headmaster Mr Weaver, Miss Davies, Miss Shilstone, Miss Bird, Mr Webber and, during the war years from London, Mr Butcher. Mr Butcher's son was called John with whom I shared a desk at school. At this time the children attending the school came from the village, and also from Coffinswell and Daccombe. They started school at five years and left at 14 to start work.

The influx of more children during the war years required more classrooms and the Constitutional Hall was used for teaching and for school dinners. It was also used for the 11-plus selection assessments for entry to Torquay and Newton Abbot Grammar schools. Mr Weaver the headmaster was also the Parish Church organist and choirmaster. He was a disciplinarian who would use the cane quite frequently on any boy that he thought deserved it.

My memories of the war years, 1939–45 were these:

Civil Defence
Stationed at Barton Hall, they would hurry through the village on their way to Plymouth and Exeter during the bombing of these cities.

Fire Brigade
The AFS (Auxiliary Fire Service) with their grey painted water pump and hoses towed by Mr Stentiford's coal lorry. They used to drive at speed along Fore Street from their shed behind the Seven Stars pub (now demolished) on their way to practise their fire-fighting at the duck pond, close to the Whitpot Mill Tea Gardens. The village boys would follow them just to watch them squirt water high into the air from their hoses. Another venue for their practice was Mr Banbury's house in Fluder Hill where the firemen would project water onto the roof.

Home Guard
They used the premises in Fore Street (now the village hairdressing salon) but previous to that Mrs Sagar's ironmongery shop. I can remember two of the Home Guard officers, Dr Colin MacVicar and Mr Vanstone who was also the Scoutmaster. On occasions the Home Guard would assemble outside Miss Newton's house at the bottom of Fluder Hill and

Fore Street, c.1932, looking south-east from the War Memorial.

march down Fore Street past the War Memorial on the way to the Parish Church for a service. My brother and myself were choirboys at this time and the robust singing of so many men was exhilarating. At the end of the war I remember the Home Guard building a large celebration bonfire on Kerswell Downs using thunder flashes as fireworks and causing injury to one bystander.

Defence Volunteers
[This was] carried out by the older men in the village. They had a corrugated-tin hut situated in the orchard in Fore Street where the garage now stands. The village boys would watch them throw a smoke grenade into the hut whereby they would crawl in through one end with their stirrup pumps, etc., and exit from another door wearing their gas masks. The sound effects were created by a man rubbing a brick against the corrugated iron. Also in this orchard was constructed a large static water tank.

Air-Raid Shelters
I watched the three brick-built air-raid shelters being constructed in what was then the school playground – the piece of ground now built upon opposite the Community Centre. The other shelter still standing was beside the Constitutional Hall in School Road. If the air-raid siren sounded the children would leave their classrooms and carry on with their lesson until the 'all clear' had sounded. Also, at the rear of the shelter in School Road was an emergency cooking unit under a tin roof (they were never used).

Evacuees
During 1940/42 a large influx of evacuees came to the village from London and Bristol to escape the Blitz on those cities. They came from an area of London, mainly Battersea, Poplar, Hackney, etc. They would arrive at Kingskerswell Railway Station with their cases, boxes, carrier bags and gas masks. The children were between the ages of four to ten years. My mother had three evacuees and three children from our family to look after. Father was away in India with the RAF.

Far left: Leslie Cheesman, Kingskerswell's British Army Champion Miler, 1955, at the RE Run at Aldershot. His time was 4.19 minutes and he was trained by Mr Jim Taylor.

Left: Lucy Goodman in her back garden, Fore Street, next to Forge Cottage. Brooklea Tea Gardens is in full view in the middle distance.

Above: Gladys Cheesman, with twins Leslie and Aubrey, early 1930s. Behind Jury's Workshop and to the right are the Tea Gardens with the wall, on the site of the Sloop.

Left: Mrs Lucy Goodman and family, Gladys, Marjorie, Leslie and Bertram, mid-1920s.

THE WAR YEARS

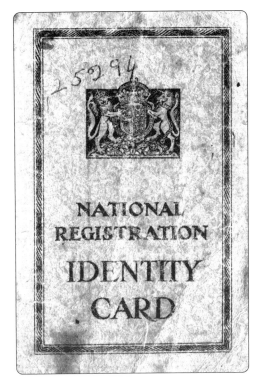
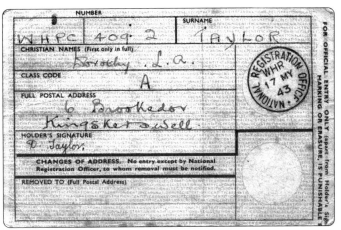

Above and top right: *Second World War National Registration Identity Card.*

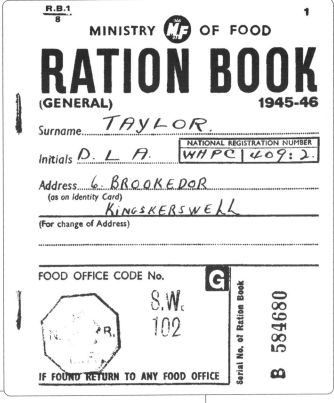

Right: *Second World War Ration Book.*

Below: *Second World War Clothing Book.*

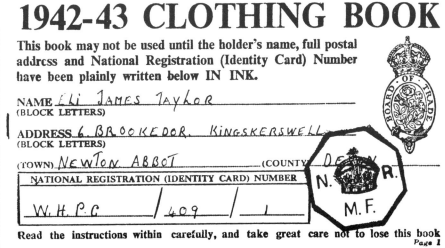

Victory celebrations invitation letter, from Jim Taylor, 10 June 1946.

THE CHILDREN OF BROOKADOR

invite you to their

VICTORY CELEBRATIONS

to be held in a field

kindly lent by Mr. Foss.

at BROOKADOR

On WHIT MONDAY,

June 10th 1946

commencing 3 p.m.

Maypole Dancing

Sports

Whist and Darts

Come and have a good time

Victory celebrations invitation card, 10 June 1946.

American Army

During 1943 the American Army arrived in this area. There was a tented army camp occupied by black American soldiers. They would hold spiritual singing evenings at their camp and the villagers were invited. Some of the men from this camp also worked the limestone quarry at Stoneycombe with the stone being transported in huge steel American Army lorries (grey-green in colour with a white painted star on the bonnet and doors). These trucks would be driven from the quarry along Fore Street and onto the main Torquay Road. The material was used to build the invasion slipways in Torquay Harbour and other defences. The children used to clamber around the 'Yanks' who were always very generous with their chewing gum and candy sweets, which we could not buy during wartime. I remember Mr Crocker who lived in Brookador – he was the quarry foreman at Stoneycombe, who once told me, long after the war, that when the 'Yanks' arrived at the quarry they blasted more rock from the quarry face in one go than the old quarry men did in a month. We used to sit on the window-ledge of the Post Office and the village would appear to shake with the blast waves and the noise.

Things We Saw and Did

[We] watched the two searchlights at night, one at Daccombe Cross area and one in the Stoneycombe area – I believe the old Army Nissen hut is still there.

A party of older children would sometimes be excused classes to help Mr Foss, the farmer, dig potatoes and store mangolds. Farmer Foss lived in the farmhouse where the Medical Centre now stands and opposite, Mr Silas Hill and his brother had their blacksmith's forge in School Road. They re-shod horses on a piece of ground beside the road.

I once remember running out of my grandma's house at 29 Fore Street to buy a large crusty loaf from Mrs Moore's bakery, one of the bakers being a Mr Brenton who lived in Yon Street. I stood in amazement on the pavement when a German bomber, which had just bombed Newton Abbot Railway Station and cottages, flew very low towards the coast.

We would collect bunches of tin foil from the fields and roads, not knowing what it was until much later. It was anti-radar detection dropped by enemy aircraft.

During some night-time air raids on Newton Abbot and Torbay, the family would cross the road from Forge Cottage to sit under Mrs Elliott's stairs for safety. We became very frightened until the all-clear sounded and the late Roly Elliott would call in from the Fire Station where he was on duty, to tell us everything was alright.

We watched a yellow RAF trainer plane spiral and crash near a field near Barton Hall.

Our mother would buy fish and chips from a mobile van which would park in Fore Street during the evening after we had gone to bed. Mother would *bring us chips which was a special treat, provided that we had behaved ourselves.*

Milk could be purchased from a pony and cart served by a lady called Norah Hill. The milk came in a large milk churn and was served with a long-handled ladle into the family milk jug.

Another treat would be to buy chocolate éclairs from Mr Hodge-Brooks' shop at the junction of Fore Street and Daccabridge Road. His wife was also a church organist at Coffinswell and tutor to any family that required piano lessons for their children. We would also form long queues at the shops whenever oranges or bananas were available, usually from Mr Moseley's greengrocery shop in Fore Street.

One night in June 1944 with our family at home we listened to a tremendous noise in the sky, which were aircraft flying to the invasion of Europe. I remember going to the front door of Forge Cottage with my mother and grandma to see, in the semi-darkness, Fore Street full of American trucks, tanks, guns and equipment on their way to their embarkation points at Torquay Harbour.

Kingskerswell Railway Station

I remember my first visit to London, going to Kingskerswell Railway Station to catch the 9.15 train. The train was pulled by a King Class engine, King George V (now in Swindon Railway Museum). The station staff were Mr Glanville, the stationmaster; and Mr Priter and Mr Tapley, station porters, who all lived in Fore Street.

MEMORIALS OF WARS

Mr Arthur Petherick lays a wreath at the War Memorial, 11 November 1956.

The earliest Kingskerswell war memorial, and the only one not commemorating a World War casualty, is that of Major Francis F. White, recorded on the gravestone of his widow in the parish churchyard. The terrible circumstances of the battle and consequent death of his young widow only ten months later represent a double tragedy.

British and other European colonisation of South Africa extended into Zululand. Kulu was the legendary ancestor-chief of the founder of the state of Zululand, north-east of Natal across the Tugela river border. The 24th Regiment crossed the river into Zulu territory to subdue the forces there but was surprised and routed by a vast army of warriors at Isandlwana (or Isandula). A surviving remnant struggled about ten miles north-west to Rorke's Drift, also on the river, where, under Lieuts Chard and Bromhead, they made an heroic last stand.

Zulu chief Cetshwayo was finally defeated in the same year and Zululand incorporated into Natal. Two decades later the Boer War claimed 20,000 British lives in three years, 1899–1902.

Official war graves for the First and Second World Wars were supplied only for those enlisted in the Armed Forces who died on active service in wartime, not necessarily abroad. Of the five official war graves in St Mary's churchyard, Kingskerswell, the two soldiers have no recorded cause or location of death listed and may have died or been killed in Britain. At least one of the two Royal Navy casualties and possibly both were in a Royal Naval Base, as HMS *Drake* was the base in Plymouth, where devastating enemy bombing raids were experienced. The RAF pilot was probably killed in direct combat with enemy forces.

Members of the Armed Forces killed abroad in action are most likely to have their war grave within one of the many war cemeteries maintained in other countries, which are sometimes visited by their relatives and friends. Of course, some of the men were also listed on a family headstone. Others who died leaving no identifiable or recoverable remains were recorded on large collective memorials either in the war arena or at home bases such as Plymouth. Some may have been listed as being residents of Kingskerswell if their family was temporarily living in the village at the time. Others included on the village memorial may have been related to those who had moved into the village and been buried there.

Kingskerswell War Memorial, Fore Street.

War Memorial service of remembrance, April 1926.

It should be noted that those serving in the Merchant Navy were civilians and, as such, did not come within the remit of the War Graves Commission. Armed Merchant ships had a quota of Royal Naval personnel in their crews. All members of the Armed Forces were expected to participate in action against the enemy whether or not their main occupation was of a combatant nature. The increasing use of air attack during the Second World War brought enemy action into many areas of this country which had previously been unaffected.

Those named on the War Memorial with no mention on a Kingskerswell grave are assumed to have been buried abroad or recorded on collective memorials in the care of the War Graves Commission.

The *Mid-Devon Advertiser* of 2 July 1921 carried an account from which the following extracts are respectfully quoted:

KINGSKERSWELL MEMORIAL HIGH CROSS UNVEILED BY SIR ALFRED GOODSON
IMPRESSIVE CEREMONY

Kingskerswell's memorial to her fallen heroes was unveiled on Sunday afternoon in the presence of almost every inhabitant of the parish. The memorial took the form of a high tapering Devon cross of Lustleigh granite, rough hewn, designed by Mr A W Searley. The cross, which with its three octagonal bases, is twenty feet high, has been placed in the centre of the village on land given in memory of Lieut. Jeffery Edwards Morton Michelmore, who fell in the war, by his mother, a former resident of the parish. [Here followed a list of the fallen men.]

The proceedings commenced with a service at the Parish Church, the flag of which was at half-mast. The ex-Servicemen paraded under ex-Lieut. C L Abbott, R.N.V.R., ex-Capt. T A Codner, R.F.A., and Warrant Officer Narramore, and marched to the church in a

Kingskerswell Memorials
1914–18

A. Baker	A.H. Clarke	G.T. Clarke
L.F. Davey	F. Furneaux	J. Furneaux
F.C. Gater	G. Gill	P.L. Heath
L.F. Hicks	A.E. Incledon	H. Kirton
A.H. Maben	M.L. Mann	H.W. Manning
G. Mitchell	J. Mitchell	R. Mortimer
F.C. Peet	A.W. Smerdon	J.H. Sharpe
H.S. Walford		

1939–45

R.C.W.H. Harvey	G.H. Hayter
P.J. Murphy	W.H. Willot.

THE WAR YEARS

body. The building was filled a considerable time before the commencement of the service. The Vicar (the Rev. G H F Fagan) conducted the short service, which commenced with the singing of the National Anthem. The hymns sung were 'Let saints on earth in concert sing' and 'O valiant hearts.'

The Vicar preached an appropriate sermon from the text, 'The place where Jesus was crucified was nigh to the city.'

In the churchyard he said they would find a few typical names representative of Jutland, Zeebrugge and the land fighting, but most of the men they were honouring were buried somewhere at the Front, or rested in the sea. The cross to their memory had been placed nigh to the village, where all could see. It would be handed over to the care of the Parish Council, and no more precious possession would ever be handed over to that Council in the days and years that were to come. They had not erected a crucifix with which their men became familiar during the war, for the crucifix did not tell the full history of the crucifixion. It spoke only of the darkness and the death. The Cross, empty, spoke of hope.

The service over, the congregation marched in procession to the cross, which was covered with a Union Jack. At the call of the Vicar, the unveiling was carried out by Sir Alfred Goodson, the Vicar dedicating the monument to the glory of God and in memory of His servants who laid down their lives in the Great War.

Sir Alfred Goodson, in a brief speech, said this beautiful memorial had been erected in honour of those men of Kingskerswell who gave their lives in the defence of their country, in defence of those glorious liberties which had been handed down to us by our forefathers. He appealed to every mother and father in Kingskerswell to teach their children of the great sacrifice made by the men whose names were inscribed on the memorial. Our old country was passing through a serious period of unrest, but he appealed to every man and woman in the parish so to rule their lives that the great sacrifice made by these men might not be in vain. The period of unrest would pass, as all such periods had passed, but it was only by work and honest work, that they could once more restore our old country to the position it occupied before the war – the envy and admiration of the whole world. Let every man and woman in Kingskerswell do his or her share.

[At this point in the ceremony, The Revd J. Charteris Johnston delivered a quite substantial and moving eulogy on the heroic sacrifice of the young men of Kingskerswell and the consequences for the lives of those left behind.]

Alderman J Taylor, C.A. (Torquay), appealed to the people of Kingskerswell, both young and old, to keep the ground on which the cross was as sacred as they did the churchyard.

The ceremony closed with the hymn 'O God, our help in ages past,' prayers and the sounding of the 'Last Post' by Pte. Walter Nicks.

A large number of wreaths were put at the foot of the cross by relatives of the fallen. Laurel wreaths were added by Pte. R Fogwill on behalf of the ex-Service men, and Dr. J R Hatfield for the War Memorial Committee. Dr. Hatfield was chairman of this committee, the other members being Messrs. A W Searley, W H Mortimer, A W Smerdon, J J Wale, S Hicks, S J Bradford, J Dart, T Dart, T Woollacott, Hon. Mrs Bingham, Miss S L Ravenscroft and Miss Rawlins. Mr A W Searley acted as secretary to the committee.

A muffled peal was rung on the church bells.

The Kingskerswell Village War Memorial Inscriptions
(A Large Stone Cross Set on Three Plinths)

'This ground was given in memory of Lieut. Jeffery Edwards Morton Michelmore by his mother.'

**To the Glory of God
and in Memory of the Brave Men of
KINGSKERSWELL who died for King and Country in the
Great War 1914–1918
'Greater love hath no man than this,
that a man lay down his life for his friends.'**

(Top plinth)

E.W. Aggett	F. Andrews	W.J. Austin	A. Baker	H.G. Braund
H. Burn	L.A. Churchill	A.H. Clarke	G.T. Clarke	H. Dart
L.F. Davey	F. Furneaux	J. Furneaux	F.C. Gater	G. Gill
R.G. Harris	P.L. Heath	L.F. Hicks	A.E. Incledon	H. Kirton
A.H. Maben	C. Mann	M.L. Mann	H.W. Manning	J.E.M. Michelmore
G. Mitchell	J. Mitchell	R. Mortimer	G. Osborne	G. Parish
F.C. Peet	J.H. Sharpe	A.W. Smerdon	H.S. Walford	E.J. Woollacott

111

THE BOOK OF KINGSKERSWELL

(Centre plinth)
AND IN THE WORLD WAR
1939–1945

K. J. Andrews   A.W. Colwell   R.J. Dart   R.C.W.H. Harvey   G.H. Hayter
P.J. Murphy   W.A. Willott

List of Memorials in St Mary's Churchyard, Kingskerswell,
linked to the First and Second World Wars
In Alphabetical Order

Grave ref. & detail	Memorial Inscription (given beneath)	Grave rating

1/4/187   Aggett (Headstone + Gravestone + Kerb)   *Family memorial*
' .... also their (George & Mary Ann Aggett) beloved youngest son, Ernest William (Aggett), Corporal Grenadier Guards, who was killed in action in France Aug. 22 1918 age 29.'

1/4/199   Andrews (Headstone)   *Official War Grave*
(RAOC insignia) '048556 Private Frank Andrews, Royal Army Ordnance Corps, 7th October 1919 aged 25.'

1/8/462   Andrews (Headstone + Kerb)   *Official War Grave*
(RE insignia) '2157987 Sapper K J Andrews Royal Engineers, 29th January 1946 age 24.' 'Father, in Thy gracious keeping Leave we now our loved one sleeping.' (Kerb Foot) 'In ever loving memory of Kenneth, beloved son of J & E Andrews, died Jan. 29th 1946. R.I.P. aged 24 years.'

1/6/342   Austin (Headstone + Kerb)   *Family memorial*
' .... Also of his (H.G. Braund) brother-in-law William James Austin, beloved son of Samuel James & Ellen Austin, who was killed in action in France March 9th 1917 aged 21 years.' 'Resting in Peace.'

* 1/1/35   Bowden (Pillow Stone on Wonacott grave)   *Family memorial*
'In loving memory of Charles E Bowden, beloved husband of Emma and son-in-law of the above (James & Amelia Ann Wonacott) lost at sea through enemy action Feb 18th 1942.' 'Resting where no shadows fall.'

1/6/342   Braund (Headstone + Kerb)   *Family memorial*
'In loving memory of Herbert George Braund (Bert), Pte. 7th DCLI, beloved husband of Ada Braund, wounded in France August 15th 1917, died January 5th 1918 aged 28 years.' 'His end was peace.' (see also 1/6/342 Austin above)

1/7/399   Burn (Headstone + Kerb)   *Family memorial*
' .... Harold John (Burn), (child of William & Anne Burn) fell in action in France Sep. 4th – 6th 1916 aged 29 years.' 'He laid down his life for his friends.'

3/7/914   Churchill (Headstone + Kerb)   *Official War Grave*
(Anchor insignia) 'L.A. Churchill, Petty Officer RE 195562 HMS Vivid, formerly HMS Marlborough, 14th April 1915 aged 35.' + 'Safely reached that blissful haven, though it's hard to say Farewell.' (Kerb; Lydia Duder Churchill)

1/15/708   Colwell (Headstone + Kerb)   *Official War Grave*
(RAF insignia) '1317864 Flight Sergeant AWJ Colwell, pilot Royal Air Force 7th April 1944 aged 32.' + 'Greater love hath no man than this, that a man lay down his life for his friends.'

N1/6/160   Crawshaw (Headstone)   *Family Memorial*
' .... Also their (Thomas & Sarah Ellen Crawshaw) eldest son, Col. CH Crawshaw DSO OBE MC killed at sea on active service 4th Aug. 1943.'

1/10/580   Dart (Headstone + Kerb)   *Family memorial*
' .... Also of Harry Dart their (John & Susan Dart) son who lost his life on HMS Defence May 31st 1916 aged 20.' 'Ever in our thoughts.'

THE WAR YEARS

Grave ref. & detail	Memorial Inscription (given beneath)	Grave rating

1/10/603   Dart (Headstone)   *Official War Grave*
(Anchor insignia) 'RJ Dart, Leading Stoker U. D/KX85156 HMS Drake 9th May 1941 aged 25.' (Pottery flower holder) 'In memory of Reggie, May 9th 1941.'

* 1/8/521   Hamilton (Headstone+Kerb)   *Family memorial*
'.... Leslie Montagu Hamilton, Pilot Officer RAF VR, missing in France May 1940.' (son of John Montagu & Effie Adelaide Hamilton)

1/5/235   Harris (Triple Plinth & Cross (collapsed) + Kerb)   *Family memorial*
'.... Also their (Felix John & Emily Mary Harris) son Reginald Gerald (Harris) killed in action Oct. 4th 1917 aged 37. Jesu Mercy.'

* 1/8/506   Hayhurst (Headstone + Kerb)   *Family memorial*
'.... Also their (John James & Sarah Elizabeth Hayhurst) son John (Hayhurst), killed in action in France 22nd May 1916 aged 20.'

1 /6/325   Mann (Triple plinth; Cross; Kerb)   *Family memorial*
'To the dear memory of Cecil Mann (8th Devons) who was killed at Loos Sep. 25th 1915 aged 22 .... '

4/5/987+8   Michelmore (Cross recumbent; Kerb; West-facing)   *Family memorial*
'.... Jeffery Edwards Morton Michelmore, his (Jeffery Edwards & Mary Eugenie Michelmore) son, Lieut. 16th East Surrey Regt.; killed in action in France April 9th 1916 aged 37'.

1/13/659   Osborne (Triple plinth + Cross)   *Personal memorial*
'In loving memory of George Arthur Osborne, Corpl. RMLI, killed at Zeebrugge April 23. 1918 aged 22 years. Faithful unto death'

1/14/681   Parish (Small Headstone with cross top)   *Family memorial*
(Child's grave of Kathleen, daughter of George & Kate Parish died 1908) '.... Also of the above George Parish who fell in action in France May 9. 1917 aged 29 years.'

3/8/923   Woollacott (Headstone)   *Family memorial*
(Anchor insignia) '.... Also Ernest James Woollacott, Chief Petty Officer, son of the above (Thomas Duder & Mary Jane Woollacott), who was killed in action on HMS Defence May 31. 1916 aged 39 years.' 'His duty nobly done'.'

Note: * The graves marked with an asterisk commemorate those who are not recorded on the War Memorial.

Zulu Wars Memorial

1/9/521   White (Headstone with integral cross; Kerb)   *Family memorial*
'On the 14th November 1879 aged 32 years, Agnes, widow of Major Francis F White, Staff Paymaster, lst Batt. HM 24th Regt., who fell at the disaster of Isandula, South Africa, 12th January 1879. In death they were not divided.'

Beating the bounds, 6 August 1923. This image shows the first assembly point in Fore Street, on the Arch, between the Seven Stars and the Lord Nelson public houses, before proceeding to Aller.

Chapter 10

Parish Events & Pastimes

Beating the Bounds, 1966
by J. Wale

On Monday 29 August (Bank Holiday) 1966, a crowd of about 150 enthusiastic villagers, young and old, gathered at Coffinswell Lane to beat the parish boundaries, all in various modes of attire for the long day's walk, some more hopeful of the weather than others, and all carrying sufficient food for the day. Mr Stanley Blackmore, dressed as a country yokel, kept the party well amused with his fine sense of humour.

The vicar conducted a short service before the start, and Mr S. Whiteway gave a short history of the beating of the bounds ceremony. Mr Peter Mills sang a special bound-beating song which he had composed himself, and Mr Peter Nalder also sang folk songs. Then, led by Mr Arthur Nicks, away we went, accompanied by some jolly tunes on the mouth-organ, and some extraordinary noises from a bugle.

At our first stop, Aller Cottages, a welcome cup of tea was provided by a Civil Defence tea van. We were met here by Mr R.S. Wills, representing the Chairman of the Newton Abbot Urban District Council. Mr Wills and Mrs J. Wale were ceremoniously bumped on the boundary stone. Also there to greet us was Dr MacVicker. Away we went again to Stoneycombe Bridge where the party was met by Mr Walke, Chairman of the Rural District Council, and Mr C. Hollamby, Chairman of the Kerswells Parish Council. Here took place more ceremonious bumping. Lunch was taken at Compton Mill by about 85 bounds-beaters. Then the party set off for Gallows Gate, where Mr W. Adams, longest-serving member of the Kerswells Parish Council, kept up an old tradition by scattering pennies to the children taking part. Here it started to rain, but on we went to our next stop at the Torquay Isolation Hospital, where we were greeted by the Mayor of Torquay, Alderman L.S.W. Howard, who

Beating the bounds, 6 August 1923. George Facey and Bill Woollacott help a young beater sense where the limit should be.

115

Left: *Beating the bounds, 6 August 1923. Beaters have not yet been beaten by the rough terrain and obstacles, near the railway line.*

Below: *Beating the bounds, 6 August 1923. The group is advancing, unhindered by traffic worries.*

Below: *Beating the bounds, 6 August 1923: time for a map check and a short rest. The squire is on the right, with rolled-up map. Mr W.H. Mortimer is next to him, with Winifred and Donald Honeywill (holding stick) before them. Mr T. Woollacott is holding open the map, with his brother Bill. Mr Burns is on the left, with trilby, fob and stick (licensee of the Park Inn). Sam Whiteway is next and George Facey with boater and dog behind them.*

PARISH EVENTS & PASTIMES

Above: *Beating the Bounds, 6 August 1923. Included in this group are: Stan Dart, Andrew Lord, Bill Mitchell, Ethel Pearce, Florence Pearce, George Facey, Samuel Bradford, Jack Matthews, William H. Wale, Silas Hill, Freddie Hill, Bill Woollacott, Bert Bibbings, squire H.L. Brown, Theo Brown, Mrs Brown, Mr Isaacs, Tom Woollacott, Eric Heywood, Alice Crocker, Miss Wallman, Dorothy Davy, Edie Mitchell, Miss Mason, Donald Honeywill, Winifred Honeywill, Ruth Coombes, Henry Best.*

Above: *Beating the bounds, 1933. Fred Crocker, ?, Norman Howard, ?, ?, ?, Billy Adams, ?, Roly Elliott, E.G.W. Brown.*

Right: *Beating the bounds, 1933. Young walkers include Cosmo Hill, Norman Howard, Arthur Nicks on the left, front row, and sixth from left, Roly Elliott.*

The commemorative mug is inscribed 'Kingskerswell Beating the Bounds, 1936' – is this a slip of the paintbrush?

Beating the bounds, Monday 29 August 1966. Jane Wale and fellow stalwarts tread warily in the boggy bit at Parson's Bridge.

Above: *Beating the bounds, Monday 29 August 1966. Councillor W. Walke, Chairman, Newton Abbot Rural District Council, is carried to a bumping point by Stan Blackmore, Dr MacVicker and A N Other, while Jane Wale secures his feet. Bob Fraser, a thirsty Roly Elliott and an appreciative crowd of boundary beaters survey the scene.*

Beating the bounds, 1990

PARISH EVENTS & PASTIMES

Itinerary

0900	New school site. Short service – the vicar
0915	Move off
0955	Underway (Coffinswell Road)
10.25	Zig-zag lay-by
1030	Aller Vale Quarry – meet Newton Abbot Civic Party
1040	Move off
1105	Langford Bridge – meet Abbotskerswell Civic Party. Coffee break
1115	Move off
1155	Maddicombe Railway Bridge
1210	Stoneycombe Bridge – Meet Ipplepen Civic Party
1210	Move off
1235	Compton Mill – Lunch break
1315	Move off
1340	Moles Cross, Ranmore Gardens – meet Marldon Civic Party
1350	Move off
1440	Kerswell Gardens – meet Torbay Civic Party
1455	Move off
1535	Kingskerswell Cross – Tea break
1540	Move off
1610	Daccombe Mill – meet Coffinswell Civic Party
1620	Move off
1640	Back at starting point....Finish

Well not quite!
A Barbeque & Barn dance will be held to the music of
'JUG O' PUNCH'
on the playing field at 1930 same day – July 9th
Entrance free Bar available

Sunday 10th – July United Civic Service

**Programme for the beating of the bounds,
9 July 1983.**

was also ceremoniously bumped on the boundary stone.

After more cups of tea we went on to Barton Hall. Here Mr Blackmore startled us all by jumping into the swimming pool fully clothed, including hob-nailed boots. He was soon followed by Alan Vooght and Peter Tibbett. But they were all very wet anyway! On we went again to Daccombe Mill to be greeted by Mrs V. Churchward, Chairman of the Coffinswell Parish Council. Now it was just a short trek to the finish at Coffinswell Lane, completing about 20 miles by 7.30p.m. Everyone was well and truly soaked; 73 people completed the route, two of the oldest being Mr W. Tozer and Mr J. Clarke, both 68 years old. There was only one casualty on the trip, Mrs E. Rendle, who unfortunately cut her leg.

During the evening a special bounds-beating social was held in the Public Hall organised by Mr Blackmore, and a whist drive at the Constitutional Hall arranged by Mr Edwards and Mr W. Hodge-Brooks. At the social specially inscribed mugs were presented to 53 children under 15 who completed a stage of the route. Mr R.W. Fraser and Mr S. Whiteway were thanked for carrying out transport operations. The whole day had been a very happy and successful occasion.

Thanks are due to a great number of people for their generosity. Members of the organising committee were: Mrs J. Wale, chairman; Mr Garrick, secretary; Mr A. Nicks and Mr S. Whiteway, joint leaders; Messrs A.R. Nicks, R.W. Fraser, W.H.R. Elliott, L.G.T. Mogridge; and Mesdames Horne, Mason and Baker.

KINGSKERSWELL HANDBELL RINGERS

After the Second World War, Fred Crocker sought out 14 handbells from villagers and, with Leslie, Aubrey and Archie Cheesman, Charlie and Tony Pain, Maurice Petherick and Jim Taylor as the original members, formed the 'Kingskerswell Handbell Ringers'. Robin Cowell and Peter Lovell joined the group later. Jim Taylor left the team in about 1947/8, and in 1952 the group became known as the 'Kingskerswell Handbell Ringing Society', captained by Mr Charlie Pain. The next leader was Mr Len Rowe and the leader at the time of writing is Mr Andrew Lovell.

The Kingskerswell society, for many years honoured with the distinction of being 'the best in the West', celebrated its silver jubilee on Saturday 8 October 1977, by which time the original eight members and 14 bells had grown to 13 members and 45 bells. The group lived up to its reputation by winning the Torbay and South West of England Music Festival (handbell class) 18 times in the space of 19 years. On Saturday 8th the society celebrated more than 25 years of success and change with a special concert at the Public Hall, Kingskerswell. In addition to its successes at Paignton, the society has played on several occasions for television and has performed at rallies in London, Leicester and Bristol, where it received encouraging praise from some of the leading handbell professionals in the country.

Its constantly changing repertoire included, during the 1970s, a modern version of 'Home Sweet Home', 'American Patrol', a selection from Gilbert and Sullivan's Iolanthe and the Minuette and Trio from Symphony No.39 by Mozart.

The society practices and performs both off-table and harmony ringing; it began harmony ringing in the 1950s when the popular Devon author Jan Stewer heard it in a Torquay hotel and arranged 'The Bells of St Mary' for the group. At that time, the ringers toured the area playing at carnivals. They have also performed for harvest festivals, and for disabled and mentally-handicapped people.

In the 1970s a new recruit was Miss Beverley Holmes, then aged 17, and formerly a player with the Gnosall Handbell Ringers, of Staffordshire – one of the top handbell ringing groups in the country at that time. Longest-serving members then were Mrs Anita Osman – one of the first three women to join the society – and her brother, Mr Andrew Lovell, who had been conductor for more than 15 years.

Handbell Ringers

St Mary the Virgin Kingskerswell, bell-ringers, late 1940s–early 1950s. Left to right, standing: Jack Wonacott, Roly Elliott, William Field, Charles Hodge-Brooks; seated: William Hill, W. Charles Gale, George Facey.

Below: *Parish Church bell-ringers, 1964. Left to right, back row: C. Doney, Len Rowe, Roly Elliott, Bert Mitchell; front: W. Wright, L. Brimson, Mrs Dunn, Charlie Bovey, Mrs Johnson, Jack Wonacott, Jim Pedlar.*

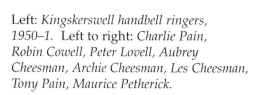

Left: *Kingskerswell handbell ringers, 1950–1. Left to right: Charlie Pain, Robin Cowell, Peter Lovell, Aubrey Cheesman, Archie Cheesman, Les Cheesman, Tony Pain, Maurice Petherick.*

PARISH EVENTS & PASTIMES

Members in 1977 were Andrew Lovell, Catherine Squire, Gillian Squire, Veronica Wright, Liz Whyte, Alan Rendle, Anita Osman, Angela Newbold, Paul Gerry, Nick Tuckett, Mike Wright, John Holmes and Beverley Holmes.

KINGSKERSWELL'S VOLUNTEERS ACHIEVE BIG AMBITION
Bernard Barnett Reports, 19 August 1961

Kingskerswell Community and Leisure Centre opening day, May 1991. Former school friends meet again outside their old school; left to right: Mrs Margaret Narramore, Mr George Moon, Miss Queenie Boon, Mrs Jane Wale.

After years of waiting and worrying, Kingskerswell's dream has come true. The new sports pavilion at the playing-field was officially opened on Saturday. There had been doubts that it would ever be built. As recently as a year ago there were some who said it wouldn't happen.

But there are determined people at Kingskerswell. Local organisations got together and discussed the project. The immediate problem was money. So they set about raising it. There were donations and profits of this year's carnival. The Parish Council helped. So did the playing-field's supporters' club; the Women's Institute; the Young Wives' Group; the cricket and football clubs; St John nursing brigade; and the Misses L. and F. Wale.

Ten years ago the playing-field was scrub. Then it was given to the Parish Council by Mr W. Adams. Now it has a fine football pitch, a fine cricket pitch and a fine pavilion. The cricket team used the old hut for the last time on Saturday. It was put up in 1932, when the club played at Coles Lane; which has now become a housing estate. During the war the hut was stored under the railway arch near the station. In 1950 progress coveted Coles Lane. The club had to move, and because there was no other pitch it disbanded until four years ago, when it moved to the playing-field. The hut moved too. Now no one seems to know what will become of the hut. It was offered to me for 30 shillings.

At the opening ceremony the chairman of Kerswells Parish Council, Mr A.W. Umpelby, said that the new pavilion was 'a great credit to the village. It should stand for many a year for the benefit of Kingskerswell.' He thanked those who had donated money towards the cost, the builders, Messrs Flowers Bros, and the architect, Mr Langler. Miss L. Wale, who opened the pavilion, said: 'My sister and I want to emphasise how indebted we are to Mr Adams for giving this site. A short while ago it was only a plan.' Mr E.J. Taylor, chairman of the Parish Council's playing-field committee, said that there had been four chapters in the development of the field.

'The first was in 1952, when Mr Adams gave the field to the Parish Council, which had the wisdom to think of youth. The second is the formation of the playing-field's supporters' club. The third is youth; the cricket and soccer clubs which have worked on the field. If you counted the man-hours put in here, the number would be astonishing. Chapter four is today. This was not an idle dream.' He thanked the Misses Wale for their gift, and added: 'I am sure that their names will go down in history.'

Mr E.W. Edwards, treasurer of the playing-field's supporters' club, presented a cheque for £159.8s. to Mr Adams. It included £109.8s. from the carnival, plus £50 from the club. Mr Adams said that the cost of the pavilion was £1,300, of which another £300 is needed for the installation of gas and water. He announced that his sister has offered to help pay for the installation of gas.

After the ceremony the cricket team went off to play cricket; and I went off to watch. The opponents were Royal Western Counties Hospital, Starcross. Kingskerswell won by 94 runs; due in no small part to John Hudson, who scored a magnificent 85 not out, then went on to take four wickets for 16. Hudson's performance must have come as something of a relief to him. In his last few matches he has scored more than 40, but has not quite managed to reach 50. On Saturday he reached 50 with the same kind of sigh that other players, including me, give when they break their duck. His score moved quickly on the unique scoreboard. Its figures come from the route indicator of a Devon General bus. It seems that from time to time the company casts off its old indicators. The club, appreciating the possibilities, moved in swiftly and snapped one up; thus ensuring that never again would there be a shortage of volunteers to work the scoreboard. Everyone likes a novelty.

The board also shows the humour of cricket and cricketers. Instead of a nought for the 'last man's' score, there is a painted duck; intended probably to surprise the victim out of despondency. Kingskerswell opened the batting with Ted Fone and Hudson who walked together to the wicket determined to turn the

Above: *Kingskerswell Cricket Club, 1922, winners of the Cup and Medals, South Devon League.* Left to right, back row: *Fred Mitchell, Harry Dart, Ern Setters, R. Mitchell;* third row: *Sam Hicks, George Facey, Fred Lake, Bob Voisey, Mr William H. Mortimer, Silas Hill, Norman Baker, W. Crocker;* second row: *A. Bristowe, W. Burn, Will Hill, Fred Lock, Sid Dart, Mr England (schoolmaster);* front: *Charlie Wonacott, Fred Hill (with furry mascot).*

Above: *Kingskerswell Cricket Club, July 1934.* Left to right, back row: *H. Whiteway, B. Mortimore, B. Castles, S. Hill, P. Foss, N. Elliott, C. Wonacott, S. Dart, L. Woollacott;* middle: *S. Ware, W. Foss, Mrs Rendle, V. Lewis, N. Hill, B. Burn, Mrs Sampson, G. Valentine, Miss Hawkins, E. Stockman, Mary Cole;* seated: *Mr Weaver, Mr William H. Mortimer, N. Stockman, Mrs Len Stockman.*

Left: *Kingskerswell Cricket Club, 1959.* Left to right, standing: *Bert Mitchell, David Luscombe, John Hawkins, Paul Venn-Dunn, Reg Edwards, Ern Jefford, Derek Woollacott, George Kidd, George Underhill, 'Buster' Brown, John Hudson, Cosmo Hill, Roly Elliott, Archie Cheesman;* seated: *Bill Fone, Derek Sharples, Ed Fone, Dick Clark, Jack Vanstone.*

PARISH EVENTS & PASTIMES

Kingskerswell Cricket Club, 1967. Left to right, standing: Les Brown, David Hagger, Derek Woollacott, E. ('Ted') Dickinson, H.E. ('Ted') Ray (president), Sid Childs, Grahame Luscombe, Harry Dart; seated: Roly Elliott, A. (Tony) Tutcher, Dennis Jenkins, A. (Bert) Mitchell, Mervyn Lancey; on grass: John Childs, Brian Woollacott.

Kingskerswell Cricket Club, 1982, Brockman Cup Winners, photographed at Torquay Cricket Ground. Left to right, standing: Michael Rowse, Dennis Jenkins, John Elliott, Barry Hayman, Barry Davey, John Ashton; seated: Peter Holme, Hugh Edwards, Willie Webster, R. (Bob) Haly (captain), Paul Mitchell, E. (Ted) Davenport, Jason Rossiter (scorer).

tables on Starcross, who earlier this season scored 225 against Kingskerswell.

The weather looked like intervening at any moment. Three times it did. As well as the rain we had another reminder that it was the start of the football season. The goalposts of the adjoining soccer ground were standing expectantly. A broadcast commentary of a football match contrasted oddly with the peace of the cricket. The crowds roared as Walsall's Taylor threatened the Sunderland goal while Ed Fone patted the ball peaceably to Starcross bowler Cann. The tension of the soccer further emphasised the slowness of the cricket, for Kingskerswell started drably. It took them 53 minutes and two wickets to score 50. Afterwards the pace livened. After losing Fone for five

and Elliott for one, Hudson and captain Bert Mitchell hit out. Mitchell hit four fours in one over off R. Cole. Hudson hit five fours in one over off Cann. The partnership put on 78 runs. Then Mitchell, trying a hook off J. Greenough, mis-hit the ball high into the air and into the hands of C. Wilton at backward short leg. Graham Luscombe, one of three brothers who play for Kingskerswell, came in to hit up the hundred with Hudson. He hit two fours, then was clean bowled by Greenough.

John Hawkins came and went, and Andre Courtaux strode to the wicket meaningly. He hit two fours, and he and Hudson began to look for runs. Unfortunately they looked rather too keenly, for with the score at 142 Courtaux was run out. In came Bob Luscombe, and he and Hudson stayed together until Kingskerswell's declaration at 173 for six. Luscombe scored five not out. Starcross' most successful bowler was Greenough, who took four for 61 in 17 overs, two of them maidens. He also bowled five wides. Cann took one for 63. Starcross looked gloomily at the pitch. The prospect was rain and defeat. Neither alternative was preferable. So they put on their sweaters, and John Hohl and Gordon Joslin walked out to open the innings...

KINGSKERSWELL SCOUT GROUP
by Richard Miller, onetime Group Scout Leader and Assistant DC, Teignbridge Scouts

The Group, with its Headquarters at Dobbin Arch on land given to us by Squire Brown (a well-known local resident), has been a part of the village scene for 50 years or more. Until recently, the Group consisted of boys and young men aged 8–18 years, but it now includes girls, and some three years ago a Beaver Section was formed for boys aged six to eight years.

In the 1970s the number of local boys waiting to join the Cub Section (8–11 years) had grown to such an extent that a second Cub Pack was formed, one being known as the 'Adams Pack', and the other as the 'Foss Pack'.

The Group has always taken an active part in both the Teignbridge District Scout activities and Devon County Scout events, and over the years took part in numerous competitions organised by the District and County, and often came away with trophies or certificates.

We have been supported throughout by an active Group committee consisting of parents and friends of the Group, the committee having raised considerable funds, which has enabled all sections to keep going. For several years, the committee held an annual fête on the old greyhound track (then owned by Sainsbury's), which is now a housing estate. Various other organisations in the village took part. Over the years we were able to attract various celebrities (including Fern Britton) to open the fête.

Left: *Kingskerswell Brownie group, 1955. Left to right, back row: Rosalie Howard, Jean Brusey, Wanda Sibley; middle: Helen Stidworthy, Mary Cole (Brown Owl), Valerie Edwards; front: Judith ?, Elizabeth Edwards.*

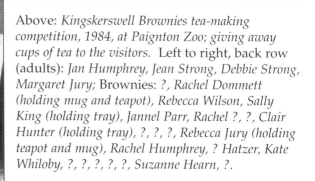

Above: *Kingskerswell Brownies tea-making competition, 1984, at Paignton Zoo; giving away cups of tea to the visitors. Left to right, back row (adults): Jan Humphrey, Jean Strong, Debbie Strong, Margaret Jury; Brownies: ?, Rachel Dommett (holding mug and teapot), Rebecca Wilson, Sally King (holding tray), Jannel Parr, Rachel ?, ?, Clair Hunter (holding tray), ?, ?, ?, Rebecca Jury (holding teapot and mug), Rachel Humphrey, ? Hatzer, Kate Whiloby, ?, ?, ?, ?, ?, Suzanne Hearn, ?.*

Kingskerswell Brownies collect a mile of pennies for charity, Saturday 22 March 1980. Emma Todd, Catherine Sharam and Sarah Gooch (with her brother) stand guard at one end of the mile.

PARISH EVENTS & PASTIMES

Throughout its existence, the group has been fortunate in having a considerable number of adults prepared to give up their time to act as leaders and helpers of the various sections. In some cases this has involved not only evening meetings but weekend activities, and camps sometimes lasting as long as a week.

The group has always taken an active part in many of the village events, and will continue to provide a grounding in the principles laid down by our founder, Lord Baden-Powell, in 1908, 'To do our duty to God and the Queen, and to help other people at all times.'

Past members of the Group, to my knowledge, are to be found throughout the United Kingdom, and indeed as residents in various parts of the world. Wherever they are, I'm sure they're making good use of the things they learnt here in the Group at Kingskerswell.

LONSEE LINKS

Following a meeting held in the Lower Church Room, Daccabridge Road, Kingskerswell, on Monday 14 September 1987, efforts were made to form our now well-established Twinning Association. The steering committee was made up of the following: chairman, Mr Philip Sproston; vice-chairman, Mr Les Haines; treasurer, Mr John Elliott; secretary, Mrs Barbara Haines; and PRO, Mrs Carol Durston. The officers then had to decide with which country we should twin. Both France and Germany were considered – in the south of either country, perhaps, as it would hopefully be warmer! After much discussion and letter writing, Lonsee in the South of Germany became the choice, as someone there spoke English! Lonsee is situated between the towns of Ulm and Stuttgart, has a population of around 5,000 people and, like us, has a school, Post Office, both a Protestant and Roman Catholic Church, a railway running through (but it also has a station), its own fire station and a marvellous sports hall with an electronic bowling alley underneath!

Following a public meeting held in January 1988 several new people became members, including Mrs Hilda MacVicker and Mrs Iris Buck, both from Coffinswell, as well as Mr Peter Fuzzey. The logo for the association is the work of Zoe Lidbury, and was chosen from designs submitted by children from the local primary school. It has recently had colour added.

A constitution was agreed and drawn up at a meeting held in February 1988. At the first AGM in 1989 there was a change of officers on the committee, Peter Fuzzey becoming treasurer and Les Haines chairman.

A letter came from the Mayor of Lonsee, Herr Gunther Merke, to Mrs Barbara Haines, requesting a meeting, and in her reply she invited a delegation to come to Kingskerswell. Seven people came in September 1988, and were shown the villages of Coffinswell and Kingskerswell, taking in the school

Signing of Kingskerswell–Lonsee Twinning Charter, 7 October 1989, Forde House, Newton Abbot. Left to right: *Mr Mike Haines, Chairman Teignbridge District Council; Herr Gunther Mack, Mayor of Lonsee; Mr Les Haines, Chairman Kingskerswell Twinning Association.*

Right: *Official Opening of 'Kingskerswellweg', Lonsee, 1997.* Left to right, at tape: *Herr Arwed Greiner; Herr Gunther Mack, Mayor of Lonsee; Mrs Margaret Jury, Chairman Kingskerswell Twinning Association.*

and churches. Then the party went further afield to the coast, and Dartmoor, now a firm favourite! On leaving, an invitation was extended for a visit from Kingskerswell to Lonsee in the spring of the following year.

The first visit to Lonsee was a resounding success, and was then followed by the signing of the charter at Forde House, Newton Abbot, on 7 October 1989, and another in Germany in October 1990. Sadly the chairman of the Lonsee committee died just after our AGM in 1991. Letters of condolence were sent to his family, and a plaque was presented in his memory.

Visits normally alternate with Kingskerswell visiting Lonsee one year, and our friends from Germany returning the next. The 'matching' of English and German families has been an incredible success. Most people stay with the same family for each visit, and strong links and lasting friendships have been formed. We have seen children grow up to become teenagers and adults. We have also seen Lonsee grow, with many new homes being built over the years. We stay in private homes, and have a very different view of the country and the way of life from that experienced by tourists. The arrangement runs on an 'exchange basis'; we do not pay our expenses in Germany, and, likewise, we pay those of our visitors when they are in England.

We received a request for a game of cricket before one visit and acquired pads, gloves, wickets and all. We even had a trophy. The trouble was, the Lonsee players had such good tuition that they began to win all the matches! We understand that they practised in Germany using a frying pan and oranges. There were quite a few spectators when we played in Germany, probably out of curiosity more than anything.

Funds for the Twinning Association are raised by a membership fee, due each May, as well as by social events, including beetle drives, quizzes, talks, barbecues, etc. The best attended is always the Christmas dinner. We had a grant of £396 for the initial visit, and since then have been successful on five occasions in obtaining a grant from the European Commission in Brussels to help with travelling and hosting expenses. These have amounted to a total of nearly £5,000. The Parish Council has also given us donations, for which we are very grateful.

Many of the German people are able to speak excellent English. There have been times when groups of us here attended German lessons. One group had been taught at school and needed to have their memories jogged, and two other groups had never spoken a word of German. They all came out of it well. The aim was a level of proficiency whereby each could hold a conversation or ask for things, either at home or while out shopping, or perhaps ask for directions in town.

The moors and the coast are very popular with most of our guests. They have also enjoyed trips to, among other places, Abbotsbury Swannery, Tintagel, Plymouth, Exeter, Barnstaple and Tiverton, where we all enjoyed a trip on a horse-drawn barge on the canal. In 2003 we visited the Eden Project in Cornwall. We obviously have time during the stay to take our guests out with us to places of interest and we also get together with other families for meals, and get to know more people better. On the last night of each visit, we have what has come to be known as the 'social evening' when all of the German and English people join together for entertainment, food, and normally dancing. The evening finishes with us all singing 'Auld Lang Syne' before getting on the bus at midnight for the journey home.

In Germany we have enjoyed trips to Neuschwanstein Castle (used in the film 'Chitty Chitty Bang Bang'), Munich, Oberammergau, Stuttgart (including the classic car area at Mercedes!), Heidelberg and Ulm. We took Teignbridge Brass, a local brass band, with us in 1992, and they played in the town of Ulm, in bitterly cold weather, and attracted quite a crowd.

We have recently celebrated our 10th anniversary on both sides of the Channel. In Lonsee we were shown slides taken over the years, and here we made a birthday cake with our logo in decoration, which was cut by the chairman of our Parish Council, Mrs Charlotte Mertens, and Herr Arwed Greiner, chairman of the Lonsee committee in Germany.

Many changes have taken place over the years. Mr Haines resigned as chairman in 1994, and was succeeded by Mr Dennis Hearn, who remained in the post until 1997, when Mrs Margaret Jury was elected; she still holds the post at the time of going to print. Mrs Barbara Haines resigned as secretary in 1991 and Mrs Maureen Haines held the post from 1991 to 1992, when Mrs Margaret Jury took on the job in which she remained until 1997, before becoming chairman. Mr Peter Fuzzey was treasurer until 1995 when Mr (Bernard) John Jury took the post until 2001. In 2003 the post is held by Dr John Broomhall. Mrs Margaret Cox is minutes secretary, but other correspondence is generally done by the chairman.

Shortly after being voted chairman, Mrs Margaret Jury found herself opening a road in a village near Lonsee. There was a ribbon to cut, a band played, and champagne flowed. The road was called 'Kingskerswellweg' – weg meaning Way. Along with Frau Ingeborg Illerhaus, chairman of Lonsee committee at the time, Margaret Jury unveiled the sign for the road, and pictures were taken by the local press. The Mayor of Lonsee, Herr Gunther Mack, who has since celebrated 25 years in the post, was also there. Herr Gunther Mack and Herr Arwed Greiner are both employed at the Town Hall in Lonsee, and have worked tirelessly during all these years on behalf of the German side of the Twinning Association. Both Herr Mack and Herr Greiner travelled to Kingskerswell to join us in our celebration of 50 years of peace since the end of the Second World War.

Sadly in 2002 Mr Peter Fuzzey, Mr John Jury and Mrs Hilda MacVicker all passed away. They, along with others, did a great deal of work to keep the association going, and are greatly missed. We hope that those of us left will enjoy many more years of friendship and exchanges.

Golden Jubilee Celebrations

In 2002 Kingskerswell marked the Golden Jubilee of Her Majesty Queen Elizabeth in glorious style, mirroring the events taking place in London. Community spirit abounded and the organisers managed to have produced something for everyone, of all ages and interests, reminding participants how wonderful it is to be part of a village community like Kingskerswell. The weather even did its bit and the sun shone down uninterrupted for the three days of events, adding greatly to the overall enjoyment.

Saturday 1 June witnessed the beating of the parish bounds, at least inasfar as they could easily be reached, and ceremonial meetings with dignitaries from the neighbouring parishes of Ipplepen,

126

PARISH EVENTS & PASTIMES

Newton Bushel Cotswold Morris Side, entertaining the village on Church Meadow, Sunday 3 June 2002, after the thanksgiving service to mark the Golden Jubilee. Dancers, left to right: Paul Conlon (foreman), Joshua Carter-Syme, Dennis Hearn (squire), Tony Jobb (bagman), Revd John Leonard, James Oram (hidden behind Tony Jobb).

Abbotskerswell, Marldon, Torquay and Coffinswell at the boundary stones. For those who wanted to enjoy the celebrations at a gentler pace a tea dance was offered at the Community Centre, whilst the more intrepid yomped through hedges, fields, mud, lanes and paths around the parish boundary.

A barn dance rounded off the evening very nicely, despite tired feet and aching muscles! Sunday 2 June brought the community together at the Parish Church for a Service of Thanksgiving, led by the Revd John Leonard, which incorporated symbols representing all aspects of the community, and this was followed by morris dancing, cream teas, and a village craft and produce market in Church Meadow.

Newton Bushel Cotswold Morris Side entertained an enthusiastic audience for much of the afternoon. The side boasts four members from Kingskerswell: Dennis Hearn, squire; James Oram; Joshua Carter-Syme; and of course the Revd John Leonard, resplendent in his Union Jack socks to mark the historic occasion. The afternoon was topped off with music from the 1950s. Monday 3 June offered music, music and still more music, to suit every taste, down in Church Meadow accompanied by a barbecue and bar. The event was very well attended with almost every square inch of grass either sat or danced upon and the bar having to send out for emergency re-supplies. Early in the afternoon, James Oram entertained the audience exchanging his morris bells for a Union Jack tee shirt and top hat and singing Sid Vicious' version of 'God Save the Queen'. The afternoon began with modern music and gradually worked its way back through the years with Jurex Jurex and Stevenson's Rocket, and culminating in a picnic on the Meadow with the big band music sounds of the 1940s, '50s and '60s of 'Tour de Force'. The celebrations were rounded off with the village beacon being lit in Church Meadow car park.

THE ROYAL ANTEDILUVIAN ORDER OF BUFFALOES

Buffaloism arrived in Kingskerswell in 1927, with a dispensation being granted to open the Sheglamacgry Lodge No.6327 on 15 September. The name of the lodge was made up from the first part of the names of four of the founder members, Brothers SHEpherd, GLAnfield, MACkrell and GRYlls. Throughout its existence the lodge held its meetings at the Halfway House Inn, the small public house on Torquay Road which reverted to a private residence when the neighbouring Hare and Hounds was built. No real record of the lodge's activities survives, but having managed to keep going throughout the Second World War it finally succumbed to a lack of support and closed in 1948.

In 1952, with support from neighbouring lodges from Newton Abbot, Abbotskerswell and Torquay, the Sheglamacgry Lodge No.8521 was opened at the Lord Nelson, Fore Street. Records show that the opening was attended by 55 Brothers, including one of the founders of the original lodge, Frank Grylls, and the landlord of the Lord Nelson at the time, Sid Bennett.

Royal Antediluvian Order of the Buffaloes (the 'Buffs'), Sheglamacgry Lodge No.6327, Kingskerswell. A founding member, Frank Grylls, in 1928, served as Provincial Grand Primo of Devon.

Kingskerswell RAOB, Brothers of the New Sheglamacgry Lodge No.8521, pictured in the 1950s. Left to right, standing: John Brown, ?, Harry Baker, W. Carpenter, Derek Unsworth, ?, Ronnie Jewel, Tommy Showell, Charlie Bartlett, George Stuckey; seated: Victor Foale, Ted Edwards, Harry Dix, Stan Blackmore, Alan Wilkes, George Smale.

To distinguish this lodge from the original, the name was changed in 1957 to the New Sheglamacgry Lodge. Following the death of the landlord and the subsequent change of licensee the lodge moved its meeting-place to the downstairs room of the Public Hall on Newton Road, formerly the village library, where it continues to meet at the time of writing.

Over the years the lodge, in addition to its benevolent work within the RAOB itself, has supported various local charities and organisations. Those within the village receiving assistance include the Scouts, St John Ambulance cadets and the Public Hall, and also individuals seeking sponsorship for worthwhile activities. Further afield the lodge has raised funds for such worthy causes as the MacMillan Nurses, Steps Cross School at Torquay, Torbay Hospital and the Children with Leukemia Foundation. In the 1960s a strong relationship was built up between the lodge and the local Sunshine Home for Blind Children, and members regularly took residents of the home to spend a day with them at weekends. In 1965, in an effort to support the home financially, members decided to put on a show in the village, and this was the beginning of the Kingskerswell pantomime, a tradition that continues to raise funds for local charities. Later the lodge became involved with the Royal National Institute for the Deaf training school at Court Grange, Abbotskerswell, inviting the students to social evenings in the lodge room and attending events at the school. Although the lodge has always had a number of members coming from outside Kingskerswell, it has maintained a strong community spirit. Organising supper dances and coach outings helped to forge links with the rest of the village. A seat was erected opposite the old primary school in memory of Bro. Harry Baker, who was a member of the Order for over 50 years. Following the redevelopment of the site the seat was replaced with one further up School Road at the entrance to the Health Centre. To commemorate the lodge's 50th anniversary in 2002, and also to mark the lodge's involvement in the life of the village, it was decided to make a further contribution to Kingskerswell amenities by replacing the dilapidated seat next to the War Memorial in Fore Street.

THE NEW FRIENDSHIP CLUB

The New Friendship Club began life in the 1970s as the Over Sixties Club, meeting once a week on a Thursday at the Constitutional Hall, now the Village Hall, in School Road, and moving the following decade to the Public Hall. There were 100 members, and a waiting-list of people wanting to join. The club held its first flower show in 1981 and enjoyed trips and holidays during the summer. Over the years the membership dwindled until, in 2001, numbers reached an all-time low. At this stage the club was given a new head, the name was changed to 'The New Friendship Club', and advertisements were placed on the boards around the village and in the *Parish Magazine*. The advertising paid off and numbers started to rise again.

Members have had a trip to Weymouth, been to the panto in Torquay and they play bingo with playing cards, along with many other games, including their own versions of 'Countdown' and 'Play Your Cards Right'. During the year Revd John Leonard visits and conducts an Easter service and a harvest service, both of which are followed by a tea, which the members provide. There is also one visiting member who attends club meetings when she is staying in Kingskerswell.

New Friendship Club, November 2000. Mrs Jan Humphrey receiving a cheque for £50 on behalf of Kingskerswell New Friendship Club from Barclays, through Age Concern, to provide new bingo clipboards. The cheque is presented by Lawrence Townsend of Age Concern.

PARISH EVENTS & PASTIMES

In 2003 membership stands at around 30 members and is growing steadily under the eye of Mrs Jan Humphrey who runs the club and was born in the village. It still meets every Thursday from 3–4p.m. in the Public Hall, members paying £1 a week, which includes payment for the photocopying, a cup of tea, biscuits, and a raffle.

THE PUBLIC HALL

The Public Hall has had many uses through the years, from Scottish dancing, pre-school and nursery, to American square dancing, keep fit and the School of Dancing. It is also used for private functions. Years ago it boasted a stage and the Amateur Dramatics Club put on plays; there was also always a dance on a Saturday night. The WI met there and the building was often the scene of fund-raising jumble sales organised by various groups. The stage was taken out to make way for new toilets upstairs and a new kitchen was put in. It was a wooden building originally, but the committee had plastic cladding put on the wood to make it last longer. They also had the car park enlarged.

KINGSKERSWELL WI

The first meeting of Kingskerswell WI was held on Tuesday 4 June 1946, in the Public Hall. There was an attendance of 50 and the elected committee was Mesdames Bayliss, Brown, Fraser, Hatfield, Higham, Jones, Lindale, Probyn and Vincent. In the early years, after the war, emphasis was placed on learning new skills and improving everyday life. There were demonstrations on all kinds of subjects, including gadgets for sewing machines, knitting finishes, and how to bottle fruit. Speakers gave interesting accounts of their experiences abroad and additional classes were held for dressmaking and handicrafts. There was a choir, drama group and dancing classes. They even entered the Newton Abbot Festival of Music and Drama.

In December 1950 the branch's membership stood at 76. Two years later members submitted entries for the August 1952 Horticultural Show in the following classes: pot of jam, jelly, salad cream, chutney, bottled fruit, fruit cake, sandwich cake, collection of vegetables, and a vase of flowers to be judged for arrangement as well as perfection.

Mrs Edith Umpleby died in January 1992 after 30 years as WI secretary. In 1995 the Devon Federation of Women's Institutes celebrated 75 years, and their banner was to be passed to every WI in the county. The accompanying book was to be signed by each President, and the mileage and form of transport employed to be noted. Abbotskerswell's Mrs Marion Sayers and Mrs Christine Lewis rode a tandem to Kingskerswell Parish Church and handed them over to President Mrs Audrey King. Mrs Dorothy McPherson then rode pillion on the motorbike of the Reverend John Leonard (Vicar) to pass them on to Post Meridian (Kingsteignton) WI.

On 4 June 1996, Kingskerswell WI celebrated its golden anniversary with a shared tea, and a cake made by Mrs Pat Burgess. Among those attending was Mrs Joyce Thorne who had been a member for 48 years. Each member received a commemorative 'gold' pen inscribed 'Kingskerswell W.I. 1946–1996'.

Kingskerswell Women's Institute celebrate their 50th anniversary, June 1996, with a birthday tea party, including ten visitors from the Haldon Group WIs. The birthday cake was made by Mrs Pat Burgess and cut by President Mrs Audrey King. Included are: 1. ?, 2. ?, 3. June Robinson (treasurer), 4. Enid McAlpine, 5. Carol Godsave, 6. Rachel Kearney, 7. ?, 8. Dorothy McPherson, 9. Kath ?, 10. Angela Grove, 11. ?, 12. Margaret Hutchinson (secretary), 13. Iris ?, 14. Merriel Grove, 15. Pearl Birley, 16. ?, 17. Audrey King (president), 18. Joyce Thorne (longest-serving member), 19. Becky Roberts, 20. ?, 21. ?, 22. ?, 23. Phyllis Crawley, 24. ?, 25. Mary Raymont, 26. Lillian Clarke, 27. ?, 28. Joan Noble, 29. Doris Moffat, 30. Kitty Edwards, 31. Lucy Hotton, 32. Wyn Rawsthorne, 33. Delphine Hucker, 34. Marjorie Anstis, 35. Pat Burgess, 36. ?, 37. ?.

Dorothy McPherson delivering the Devon WI's 75th anniversary banner with Revd Leonard, 1995.

'Little Jack Horner', summer 1929. Left to right, back row: Louis Triggs, Henry Hall, Viola Powling, Len Matthews, Albert Williams, Sybil Garrett, Bill Owen, Becky Mortimore, ?, Victor Aggett, Evelyn Wonacott; third row: Cyril Sampson, Peggy Smale, Ronald Channing, Ern Wyatt, Peggy Andrews, ?, Cyril Martin, Dennis Murphy, Mary Gully, Arthur Nicks, Roland Elliott, Ken Sampson; second row: Freda Dart, Jack Terrell, Grace Dart, Mary Cole, Percy Drake, Joyce Germon, Donald Pack, Winnie Brown, Bessie Stentiford; front: Clara Butt, Harold Dart ('good boy'), Marjorie Mitchell, Ted Stentiford, Iris Brown.

Another school performance on the same day as 'Little Jack Horner', 1929. Left to right, back row: Peggy Andrews, Viola Powling, Grace Dart, Bessie Stentiford, Winnie Brown, Evelyn Wonacott, Becky Mortimore; middle: Marjorie Mitchell, ?, Peggy Smale, Clara Butt; front: Mary Gully, ?.

PARISH EVENTS & PASTIMES

Kingskerswell pantomime, Cinderella, 21 January 1965. Left to right, back row: Tommy Showell, Lynda Spriggs, Mary Underhill, Julia Fletcher, Joyce Hern, Julia Brown, Elizabeth Edwards, Carol Underhill, Rena Brown, Kay Brown, George Jefford; middle: Ronnie Jewell, Stan Blackmore, Terry Moon, Hilary Coles, Nancy Underhill, Linda Evemy, Linda Blackmore, Kenny Fletcher; front: dancers from Castle School of Dancing, Torquay.

Left: *Kingskerswell pantomime, Cinderella, 1992. Left to right: Katrina Crowley, Alan Rendle, Jean Cooper, Stan Blackmore, Elaine Townhill.*

Right: *Eileen Cann, in charge of make-up for 25 years, applying the grease paint to Tom Kennedy.*

Presentation of £600 each to 'Friends of Rowcroft' and 'Malcolm Sargent Cancer Fund for Children', raised by the Kingskerswell panto production of Rumpelstiltskin, *3 April 1993.*
Left to right: Gerry Palmer, ?, ?, Stan Blackmore.

131

Maypole dancers, c.1933. Left to right, back row: Mr Fred Crocker, Peggy Andrews, Phyllis Field, Violet Whitfield, Mrs Crocker; third row: Peggy Smale, Alice Dart, ?, Hazel ?, ?, Joan Dart; second row: Grace Dart, Winnie Brimicombe, Freda Dart, ?, Marjorie Mitchell, Marjorie Nicks, Joan Rees, Clara Butt, Evelyn Wonacott, Marjorie Knapman; front: Iris Brown, Doris Wonacott, ?, ?, Joyce Smale, Phyllis Tozer, Gwen Nicks, Mary Cole, Dorothy Burn.

Left: *Maypole dancing when it rains, c.1935, in the Constitutional (now 'Village') Hall. The dancers include Joan and Audrey Pauls, Doris Wonacott, Gwen Nicks, Joyce and Elsie Hayter, Margaret Fields, Margaret and Betty Woollacott, Evelyn and Gladys Knapman, Phyllis Dugger, Joyce and Connie Germon, Phyllis Tozer, and Sheila Payne.*

Maypole dancing on Foss' Field, Brookador, c.1946. This field has since vanished under housing.

Maypole dancers, on the greyhound track, c.1946.

PARISH EVENTS & PASTIMES

Magnificently decorated horse-drawn float carrying young maypole dancers, c.1920s. The horse was lent by Stentiford's Farm.

Fred Crocker with maypole dancers and a float drawn by a horse from Stentiford's Farm, c.1935. It was decked out in purple and gold.

Left: Aller Vale Football Club, Winners of the Devon Junior League Cup Competition, 1893–4. Left to right, standing: A. Bowden, J. Hore, A.F. Whiteway, Samuel Bradford, A. Lee, George W. Bond, Frederick Nix; middle: Thomas H. Dart, Thomas Evans Causey (captain, holding football), Samuel Hicks (sub-captain), Thomas Woollacott (hon. sec.); front: George H. Causey, Albert Howard, Albert Redaway, William Howard. At least six of these players worked in Aller Vale Pottery.

Right: Kingskerswell Colts, mid-1940s. Left to right, back row: Jim Taylor, Charlie Pain, Fred Crocker; centre: Phillip Wise, Matthew Short, Tony Pain, Les Cheesman, Alan Crocker, Aubrey Cheesman, ? Powling, John Ridgeway, ? Gater; front: John Squires, Rod Dart, Bob Crump, Bernard Hill, Bill Tozer (with football), Godfrey Knapman, Maurice Petherick, Chris Powling, Chris Brailsford.

Left: Kingskerswell Rovers AFC, early 1950s. Left to right, standing: Syd Crocker, Bill Mitchell, Reg Wyatt, Sam Whiteway, Roland Hancock, Ivor Evans, Leslie Watson (played goalkeeper for Huddersfield), Brian Munro, Roy Moon, John Fogwill, Jack Swann, Les Wyatt, Keith Dart, Edgar Roberts, Ern Wyatt, Alan Parnell, Jim Quance, Bert Mitchell, Les Palmer, Arthur Thorne, Percy Drake, Mr Ridgeway; front: Percy Moon, Bob Wyatt, Rob Bailey, Bill Owen, George Moon, Bob Fogwill, Roland Elliott with football, Cosmo Hill, Les Parnell, Walt Brooking, Keith Lee, Bill Knapman, Charlie Brooking.

PARISH EVENTS & PASTIMES

Below: *Kingskerswell Colts, 'Jones Cup', mid–late 1940s.* Left to right, back row: *Mr Charlie Pain, Dennis Squires, Bill Tozer, Revell Green, Tony Pain, Mr Jim Taylor, Les Cheesman, ?, Aubrey Cheesman, Maurice Petherick, ?, Mr Fred Crocker;* middle: *Mr Archie Cheesman, Bob Crump, Chris Berrisford, Mr Jones holding cup, Terry Lock, John Ridgeway, Mr Norman Gater;* front: *Mike Graham, Phillip Evans, Rodney Dart, Mike Knapman, Matthew Short, Alan Crocker, Graham Oakley, John Titcombe.*

Above: *Kingskerswell Colts playing for the 'Jones Cup', mid-1940s, on the playing-field, now the Carswells estate.* Left to right, back row: *Les Cheesman, Mike Knapman, Dennis Squires;* third row: *Mr Jones with cup;* second row: *Terry Lock, Bob Crump, John Titcombe;* front: *Mike Graham, Chris Berrisford, Rodney Dart, Revell Green, Graham Oakley.*

Left: *Kingskerswell Colts, early 1950s, 'Jones Cup' presentation.* Left to right: *Revell Green, Mr Jim Taylor and Mr Fred Crocker look on as Phillip Wise receives the Jones Cup from Mrs Edith L. Petherick.*

Above: *Kingskerswell Colts, 1952–53.* Left to right, standing: *Mr Fred Crocker, Mr Arthur Petherick, Bernard Hill, Dennis Rapson, Phillip Evans, Phillip Wise, Revell Green, Mr Jones, Mr Jim Taylor;* front: *John Moon, Tom Minchinton, Stuart MacDowell, Brian Gibbins, Alan Bastow, Brian Bastow, Terry West.*

Left: *Kingskerswell Colts AFC, final, South Devon Minor Cup Winners, 1952–3 season. Mrs Dorothy Taylor presents the cup to Brian Gibbins, team captain.*

OFFICIAL PROGRAMME
SOUTH DEVON MINOR FOOTBALL LEAGUE
THURSDAY, 23rd APRIL, 1953

Upton Athletic Reserves
v.
Kingskerswell Colts
MINOR CUP FINAL

Upton Athletic Res. Colours: Gold & Blue Squares

RIGHT   A. RIDOLFO   LEFT
2 B. MANTLE   3 J. CLARKE
4 A. FLETCHER   5 R. DAVEY   6 L. PEARCE
8 L. LAWRENCE   10 W. CROCKER
7 A. McGOVERN   9 M. BULEY   11 G. MEREDITH

Referee   Mr. W. Davey   Linesmen— Mr. Lumby / Mr. Sanderson

11 A. BASTOW   9 McDOWELL   7 J. MOON
10 B. BASTOW   8 T. MINCHINGTON
6 R. GREEN   5 B. GIBBINS CAPT.   4 B. HILL
3 P. WISE   2 D. RAPSON
LEFT   P. EVANS   RIGHT

Kingskerswell Colts   Colours: Amber

South Devon Minor Football League
MINOR CUP FINAL
PLAINMOOR
THURSDAY, APRIL 23rd
Kick-off 6.30

UPTON ATHLETIC
RESERVES
v
KINGSKERSWELL
COLTS

Presentations by Mrs E. J. Taylor

Admission—Ground and Stand 1/-   Children 6d.

Official programme for the South Devon Minor Cup final, 23 April 1953.

Official poster for the South Devon Minor Cup final, 23 April 1953.

Jim Taylor with Mike Sangster, who in 1956 played for Kingskerswell Colts AFC.

Kingskerswell Rovers AFC, March 1967. Left to right, standing: Dennis Rapson, Roger Marshall, Victor Coombs, Bobby Luscombe, Roger Moon, Clive Downer; front: Grahame Luscombe, ?, Brian Woollacott, Clifford Crump, Terry Moon.

PARISH EVENTS & PASTIMES

Left: *Ladies' Football Team, Carnival, 21 July 1951. Referee: Mr Charlie Bartlett (brave man!); left to right, back row: Dorothy Fogwill, Pam Howard, Joy Howard, Beryl Searle, Mary Short, Mary Tozer; front: Mrs Edie Bond, Maureen Brown, Doreen Holmes, Beryl Pugh, Irene Wakeham.*

Right: *Ladies' Football Team, Mothers, Carnival, 21 July 1951. Referee: Mr Charlie Bartlett; left to right, back row: Mrs Scott, Mrs Fogwill, Mrs Jones, Mrs Pugh, Mrs Wyatt, Mrs Cann; front: Mary Cole, Mrs Stentiford, Mrs Stidworthy, Mrs Bartlett, Vera Pillage.*

Left: *Summer 1949, the winning team against Totnes. Left to right: Roly Elliott, ?, Fred Birley, ?, Pearl Birley, Bill Bovey.*

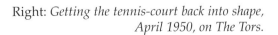

Right: *Getting the tennis-court back into shape, April 1950, on The Tors.*

Left: *Bowling for the pig, coronation carnival, 1953. Left to right: ?, Dr MacVicker, 'Nobby' Edwards, Harry Bartlett, Dilys Petherick bowling, Jabez Petherick, Joan Brenton, ? and baby ?, Shirley Ley, Mrs Brown, ?, ?, ?, ? Tozer, Bert Woollacott, ? (pipe smoker), Reg Gale, ?.*

Right: *Revd and Mrs Rowe with the car presented five months earlier to the vicar by his friends, for 21 years' service as vicar of Kingskerswell, Sunday 14 August 1962.*

Left: *Revd Alan Rowe, harvest festival time, 1960s.*

Right: *South Devon Model Off-Road Club, April 1996, at the Kingskerswell racetrack, in the old Foredown Lane Quarry. After a difficult period resulting from the outbreak of foot and mouth, the club has, since early 2002, re-formed as Teignbridge Radio Auto Klub.*

PARISH EVENTS & PASTIMES

Above: *Kingskerswell Liberal Party outing to Gough's Caves, Cheddar, c.1925. Left to right, standing, back row: Frank Dart, ?; standing, centre: Frank Gale (from Coffinswell), Jack Dart (with pipe), Eddie Bond, Mrs Best, Mrs Nicks, Walter Nicks, Mrs Davy, Mrs Clarke (lived in Water Lane), Mrs ?, Mr ? Millward (village photographer); seated: Mrs Brimicombe, Tom Crocker, Fred Crocker, Frank Milverton, ?, Mrs ? (with walking stick), Mr George Brimicombe, driver. The vehicle appears to be left-hand drive.*

Right: *Village Victorian mini-market, 7 August 1993. Mrs Vi Rowe in costume.*

Village Victorian mini-market, 7 August 1993. This was a day for dressing up. Pictured are Revd and Mrs John Leonard and family.

Kingskerswell Village Hall, School Road, originally the private theatre on Lord Clifford's Ugbrook estate.

139

Above: *Coronation day on the playing-field, and the presentation of deeds by Mr William (Billy) Adams to Mrs Hatfield, Chairman of Kingskerswell Parish Council. Also present are Jim Taylor and Dr MacVicker.*

Below: *Bowling for the pig, Conservative fête at the Constitutional (now 'Village') Hall, 1962. Left to right: Mrs Brightman, Mrs Taylor, Dr Colin MacVicker, Mrs Davies (née Brenton), Joyce Hern, ?, ?.*

Above: *Samuel Hicks (1895–1974), Jane Wale's father, with the large granite stone which he donated to the village from his farm at Venton, Widecombe, for the W. Adams commemorative plaque.*

PARISH EVENTS & PASTIMES

Left: *One of the last Carnival Queens in Kingskerswell, 20 May 1961.*
Left to right, back, standing: *Tommy Showell, Stan Blackmore, Ted Edwards, Gerry Palmer, Norman Lloyd-Roberts*; middle: *? Voysey, Petal Conn (holding Crown), ?*; front: *Joy Cousins (attendant), Linda Blackmore, Christine Dodd (attendant).*

Right: *The coronation year Carnival Queen, 1953. Left to right: Arthur Petherick, Shirley Ley (attendant), S. Pain, Dilys Petherick, Joan Brenton (attendant).*

Below: *Kingskerswell Village Band, c.1890. Unfortunately, naming individuals has so far proved impossible.*

141

Left: *Girl Talk 1906 style – Edwardian text messaging – addressed to Miss G. Hill at 4 Christchurch Terrace, Warminster, Wilts, this card from E. Bovey carries hints for a future event. Emmeline (Emily) Bovey is listed as being 18 on the 1901 census. Her friend Gwennie (Gwendoline) Louise Hill, daughter of Silas Hill, blacksmith of Kingskerswell, marries William Harold Low, on 17 September 1917. William, at 27, three years younger than Gwennie, is a private in the Wiltshire Regiment in Warminster. Emily asks cryptically 'do you see anyone belonging to you on this card?' On the 1901 census, 14-year-old Gwennie has three brothers; Silas, 17, Fred, 16, and William, 10, all of whom may well be the focus of Emily's question. The scene on the card appears to be a football match (Aller Vale?) on Bovey's Field, now the Carswells estate.*

Right: *Kingskerswell Townswomen's Guild, 26 February 1999, at the planting of an oak tree in Church Meadow to mark the movement's 70th anniversary. Left to right: Norman Hern, Vi Rowe, Betty Legge, Becky Roberts, Elsie Oulton, Christine Collins, Jan Humphrey, Zena Honeywill, Barbara Williams, Freda Newland, ?, Barbara Hewitt, ? and Revd John Leonard look on while Chairman Jean Cooper and President Charity Rosenburgh wield the shovel.*

Below: *Kingskerswell ladies' outing, gathered outside the Seven Stars, Fore Street, c.1952. Left to right, standing against coach and wall: Mrs Nicks, Mrs Barnes, Mrs Wakeham, Mrs C. Moon, Mrs Webber, Betty Moon (née Woollacott), ? (partially obscured), Mrs Selway, ?, Mrs Flo Harris (in profile), Mrs Phillips (landlady Seven Stars), ?, Mrs Norah Cornish (partially obscured), ? (Mrs Phillips' sister), Mrs Edie Milverton; middle: Mrs Woollacott, Mrs Dart, Mrs Dyer, Kit Warman, Mrs Flo Nix; front: Mrs Bratcher, ?, Mary Cole (Mrs Hancock), Mrs Milverton; foreground: Violet Steer, Mrs Griffiths.*

PARISH EVENTS & PASTIMES

Right: *St John Ambulance Brigade, 1953. Left to right, back row: Nan Hartnell, Audrey Paul, ?; front: Jean Brusey, Mrs Umpleby, ?, Joy Howard.*

Above: *St John Ambulance Brigade, annual inspection, 1954. Left to right: Joy Howard, Miss Haskins, three county officers, Mrs Umpleby.*

Above: *Ladies' Darts Team, coronation, 1953. Left to right, back row: Kit Warman, Gwen Pike (née Wyatt), Eileen Bishop, Flo Harris, Mrs Webber, Mrs Cornish; seated: Mrs Bunce, Mrs Oliver Stentiford, Mrs Norah Cornish, Mrs Bessie Selway.*

Left: *Kingskerswell skittles team, Newton Abbot League, in the Public Hall, mid-1960s. Left to right, standing: Phil Evans, Dennis Rapson, Gerry Palmer, Dave Luscombe, Cliff Brightman; front: Derek Woollacott, Ivor Evans, Les Brown.*

Seven Stars outing, c.1924. Left to right, standing: Driver, ?, ?, Aaron Cole, Jim Ridley, Tom Tucker, ?, ?; seated: ?, Bert Lowe (proprietor, Seven Stars), ?, ?, ?, ?, Fred Crocker (junr), Stan Howard, Sam Collis, ?, Harry Bond, Jack Tyrell (senr). Also present were: Jim Beare, George Osborne, Tom Woollacott, Jack Tozer, ? Hill (brother of Silas).

143

Left: *Charlotte Mertens receiving, from Chancellor Vestey, her insignia medal and certificate, at St John's Church, London. Sanctioned by the Queen, Charlotte received the award promoting her to Officer of the Most Venerable Order of the Hospital of St John of Jerusalem, in recognition of 30 years' dedicated service to Devon's St John Ambulance Brigade.*

Right: *Popular and happy couple Jane Hicks and John Wale, St Mary the Virgin, Kingskerswell, 1943.*

Below: *Afternoon tea in the garden of Holmleigh, Fluder Hill, July 1923. Left to right: Mary Ravenscroft, mother pouring tea, Sybil Laura Ravenscroft.*

Chapter 11

PERSONALITIES: A MISCELLANY

CHARLOTTE MERTENS

Charlotte Mertens moved to Kingskerswell in 1980 from Newton Road, Torquay. She worked as a Health Visitor at the Albany Street Surgery, Newton Abbot, for 25 years and before that was a part-time lecturer in nursing at South Devon Technical College. She trained at Torbay Hospital as a Senior Registered Nurse and studied obstetrics at Exeter Hospital before going on to college at Plymouth, Cheltenham and Torbay.

Charlotte joined the St John Ambulance in 1961, starting at the bottom of the ladder as a Nursing Officer and ending up as a County Nursing Officer for the county of Devon. As a result of 30 years of dedicated voluntary service, Her Majesty the Queen sanctioned a special award for Charlotte and she was summoned to London where she was presented with an insignia medal and certificate at St John's Church.

Charlotte is also a parish councillor and a school governor at Milber School in Newton Abbot.

In 1994, together with John Petherick, Charlotte started the Sharing Care Support Group at Kingskerswell, a patient-support group based at the Health Centre, whose volunteers help people with shopping (or sit with them whilst a partner is away doing this task) and prescription collection. Charlotte explains more about the group:

In the summer of 1993 I attended a Voluntary Service Meeting, on behalf of the Parish Council. The subject on the agenda was the setting up of volunteer groups in the community, to help with visiting the elderly and disabled. We were given information on how to start such a group. I contacted the doctors and staff at the Kingskerswell Health Centre, to find out if they were interested in this venture. I found that they would very much support it. I asked John Petherick, a fellow parish councillor, to attend a 'follow-up' meeting with me and discuss the feasibility of starting a group in Kingskerswell. At the following Council meeting, we reported our ideas and suggestions to the full Council. We were promised that the Parish Council would help with the insurance, if we were successful in starting a group, and if we raised some funds ourselves. A public meeting was held at the Kingskerswell Health Centre and we were able to sign up enough volunteers

to form a steering committee. We arranged more meetings and planned the publicity, with articles in the church and school magazines, and the display of posters all around the village. Members of our steering committee attended many meetings all over Devon, to gather information. Eventually we were ready to recruit our first volunteers. The staff at the Health Centre had already supplied us with names of patients who would possibly benefit from a visit by a volunteer. The next step was to form a working committee. A chairman, secretary and treasurer were elected and another public meeting arranged at the Health Centre. We organised a cheese-and-wine evening, which was well attended, and we were able to sign up several volunteers. We designed various forms, such as application forms for clients and volunteers; these were left at the Health Centre for easy access and soon we were able to start to function. The purpose of our group was to help people in our community. Local volunteers who had the time and experience were helping patients in our village. The group was based at the Health Centre and liaised with the staff there. Our aim was to provide a service in support of that instigated by the primary Health Care Teams. The type of tasks carried out by the 'Sharing Care Volunteers' are many and varied and include sitting with patients, befriending those with no close relatives, collecting prescriptions and shopping. Anyone who feels that the group might be able to help, or who would like to join us, should contact the Health Centre.

ROMANY JONES

Romany Jones Café, a well-known local landmark, has a varied and interesting past, details of which are difficult to obtain, but some key dates and facts have been recorded. For example, it is known that the wagon is primarily constructed of seasoned Russian pine boarding, tin cladding and an iron chassis and running gear. It was built by a company called Orton & Spooner, well known for this type of work during the latter part of the nineteenth century. Dated at 1890, Romany Jones would have been commissioned as an accommodation caravan for one of the senior members, or even perhaps one of the owners, of a travelling fair. Due to its length (over 33 feet long), it would have been a sizeable purchase and affordable

145

by only the established fairground members. Around 1900 there were many such travelling fairs which enjoyed great popularity. One such was located on Paignton Green in the grounds of the Redcliffe Hotel, and for many years was called Handcocks Living Picture Palace, which was later shortened to Handcocks Fair. It was originally invited to Paignton to complement the Paignton Regatta and proved so popular that it stayed! One can imagine Romany Jones being towed by a team of four or six shire-horses or even a couple of elephants perhaps, and later, by steam traction engine.

In 1906 government legislation prevented the use of solid rubber tyres on the new tarmacadam highways, which forced such vehicles off the roads and consequently they were either dumped or sold off to farmers. It is believed that Romany Jones was abandoned at the Goodrington railway sidings formerly belonging to the GWR; here rail and freight workers would use it for tea and rest breaks.

In 1927 a local entrepreneur and caravan-site owner purchased Romany Jones from the GWR for an undisclosed sum, and had it towed to Louville Holiday Park at Higher Clennon, Goodrington, where it was used as a honeymooners' caravan (named 'Charmaine') for over 30 years, except during the war years, when the site was commandeered to billet US soldiers for the Allied effort.

The site that neighbours it at the time of writing was the original road into Torbay, which was straightened c.1960, thereby creating a lay-by. Romany Jones was on the original road as a snack wagon available to passing traffic, but was ordered to move in 1974 when it became illegal to sell food on the newly appointed 'A'-road-status highway. The caravan was then hauled by block and tackle to where it stands in 2003.

JANE WALE

I was born at Cockwood in the parish of Cofton in 1921. Five years later, the family moved to Daccombe in Coffinswell, then in 1933 to Kingskerswell, where our family can be traced back in parish records to 1703. Here I lived at Foredown Farm with two sisters and a brother. I was the eldest, and attended the village primary school for a short time before going on to other schools in the area and finishing with a commercial course. After a spell working for Chanelle in The Strand, Torquay, from 1937, I left in 1940 to train to be a nurse working at Dawlish Cottage Hospital, qualifying as an SEN.

I used to walk to school from Daccombe to Homelands Central School in Torquay. After the family move during my early teens I would catch the train to Torre and then use the tram to Babbacombe. In so doing I met my future husband John Wale at Kingskerswell Railway Station. John's family originally came to the village in 1820, and he lived at

Coldstray Farm in Yon Street. Before long he asked to meet me from Night School in Torquay where I was studying bookkeeping, and he would accompany me home. John was four years older than me and I looked no further, being very taken with him, and we married in 1943.

A century before, in 1849, our two families of Hicks and Wale had formed an earlier link in the marriage of a great-aunt of John's to a great-uncle of mine. A son, John Wale Hicks, was born and baptised in Kingskerswell Church, and he later became Bishop of Bloemfontein in South Africa.

At the old school in the village Miss Birley and Miss Shepherd ran the County Library, where aged 16 I helped in the evenings. There were then big cupboards in the first room on the right from the main entrance and the library books were stored here. I used to take them out of the cupboards, put them out on the tables and desks, and at the end of the evening put them back again. Here again John used to meet me and accompany me home. I had to be in by 9.00p.m. and John would be invited in as well. He was articled to a firm of architects in Devon Square, Newton Abbot, but because of the war was not able to complete. Because of a farm accident with his hand when John was three years old he was also unable to join the Forces. He got a job in T.P. Bennett's and helped set out the first runway at Heathrow Airport for use by the bombers in the Second World War. He got little sleep at night because of Doodlebug raids, and V1 and V2 rockets homing in on London.

After the war, John joined Staverton Builders working on the restoration of Dartington Hall and we both enjoyed having tea there with the Elmhirsts once a year. Our home Redhill was built in 1951. Sadly John died in 1989. I have sustained an active interest myself in village life in Kingskerswell, joining the Mothers' Union in 1944 and still go to meetings. I was elected a parish councillor in 1965 and served on the Council for ten years. With Margaret Sheffield and Eileen Cole, I started a Young Wives Group and in 1985 I became a churchwarden.

My father, Samuel Hicks, gave from his farm at Ventor, Widecombe, a large granite stone to Kingskerswell, for use on the playing-field. The Parish Council bore the cost of transport and it was placed on site in the early 1950s where it now bears a plaque commemorating Mr W. Adam's generous gift of the playing-field to the village. In 1838, the Tithe Map showed these fields bearing the names 'Lower Yon Street', 'Higher Yon Street', and 'Martins Kings Meadow'.

Coldstray Farm was left to John by his father when he died in 1943. It was let, however, to George Webber who rented 32 acres, part of which ran alongside Edginswell Lane. Some of the field names I remember from Coldstray Farm are 'Gourders', 'Second Gourders', 'Great Gourders' and 'Lane Gourders'. John sold Coldstray Farm in the 1980s because of the

146

proposed Kingskerswell bypass route which threatened to affect the land.

THE MISSES RAVENSCROFT

In the early 1920s the Ravenscroft family lived in 'Holmleigh', 2 Fluder Hill, Kingskerswell. The father was a retired judge from India. They had livery staff, with horse and carriage, and were indeed typical of the gentry of the day. The two daughters, Miss Sybil and Miss Mary Ravenscroft, used to walk down through the village wearing long dresses and straw hats and carrying silver canes; one was obliged to step off the pavement as the sisters passed by.

In December 1899, Miss Ravenscroft took the part of Margaret Woodleaf, the wife of Harold, in a 'Comedietta' by A.M. Heathcote presented as part of a 'Musical and Dramatic Entertainment' for the benefit of the Parish Institute and Lighting Funds. The part of Mrs Percy, Harold's sister, was played by Miss M. Ravenscroft.

The father of the girls had stipulated as a condition of his will that neither should marry – if they did so their inheritances would immediately be forfeited and consequently neither Sybil nor her sister Mary married.

One day Mr Arthur Petherick of the Post Office bought a car and parked it outside on the road, announcing that it was for hire. This was the first car which the Misses Ravenscroft travelled in; Mr Petherick and his son Jabez were the only people to drive the family about.

Miss Mary Ravenscroft was a very accomplished artist and she would often ask Mr Petherick to drive them out onto the moors where she would sometimes paint a scene.

Sybil died in May 1954 aged 89 and her younger sister Mary died in November 1966 at the age of 97. Next to their grave in St Mary's churchyard is that of Edward Ravenscroft, a priest, who died in January 1944 aged 82.

RENÉ GALLANT, 1906–85

Kingskerswell is a community which can be justifiably proud of its gallant war heroes whose names are commemorated on the War Memorial in Fore Street – young men in their prime

Kingskerswell's Belgian War Hero, René Gallant, and his wife Louise, in their garden at Brook Cottage.

with their future lives and prospects before them, yet cruelly snatched away, not only in the defence of their own country and values, but also in the dutiful defence of other countries and values abroad. These young men of Kingskerswell did not return to tell their tale.

The village, however, was by fortunate circumstance honoured with the presence of a live war hero from one of those far-flung countries, and who did escape the ultimate sacrifice against all odds. René Gallant lived out his last years with his wife Louise in Brook Cottage in Stoneycombe and was a familiar and respected figure in Kingskerswell.

Colonel René Gallant of the Belgian Air Force, awarded the Croix de Guerre avec Palme and many other decorations, died on 22 February 1985, peacefully in his sleep at his own home. This was a sharp contrast to the sufferings, privation and savage cruelty his body had endured at the hands of the Gestapo in Dachau Concentration Camp. He was one of the successful few to escape from Dachau, and by a cruel twist of fate later endured hardship for many months more in General Franco's gaols.

Invalided out of the Air Force in 1949, René was later presumed to be dead and was X-rayed by doctors who were astounded to find that he was still breathing. Alive he most certainly was, and he lived another 36 years, although it was thought that he would not last longer than a few months. If asked how he was, René would always answer, 'I survive'. With the passage of time, as one of Nature's great survivors, he was thankful for each day that came.

His great courage and iron will in adversity were recognised effectively in the award of the Croix de Guerre. This was given with a citation which included the words:

... he committed himself entirely, both in intelligence work and in action, to a relentless struggle against the enemy... he fulfilled with great distinction, all the missions which were assigned to him… he gave proof in the carrying out of his duties, of an heroic indifference ('insouciance') to danger, and of a devotion to duty which knew no limit.

No wonder then that not even barbarous Nazi guards could hold such a man.

René's extraordinary war service is a long story which is told more fully in the *Transactions of the Torquay Natural History Society*, but scientific knowledge became his lifelong sphere of interest. With a mathematical and engineering background, he acquired a consuming interest in meteoric impact studies, resulting after 15 years in the publication of his book *Bombarded Earth* (1964). This pioneering study never received due recognition but others have borrowed from it without acknowledgement. René continued his research to the end. One astronomer noted that Gallant 'was ahead of his time', and 'twenty years too soon' was the observation of one academic geologist. His work contributed to his election to a Fellowship of the Royal Astronomical Society, recognition due indeed.

René first arrived in London in 1942 as an officer, penniless and a physical wreck, and with hardly a word of English except for 'cheers!' Twenty years later he returned to London, to find the books and scientific journals he needed. He found, however, more than books, meeting his future wife, Louise, who brought him to Devon. This represented a dramatic turning point in his life, and his new partner, comrade and collaborator, with loving care and deep understanding, and a strong will and discipline to match his own, gave him more years of an intensely happy life than he could ever have expected. A competent and thorough archaeologist in her own right, the late Louise Gallant, in collaboration with Norah Luxton and the late Morris Collman, carried out a comprehensive survey of the archaeological heritage of Kingskerswell.

René never forwent the beauties of his native Belgium, visiting it every year, yet also finding deep satisfaction in being an honorary Devonian. Improved health, peace and a wide circle of friends were comforts he cherished here and he owed the Torbay area a great deal. In return his good will, proverbial generosity and infectious cheerfulness touched everyone he met.

Kingskerswell's 'Grand Old Man of Peace'

William Henry Mortimer was one of those rare people whose very character and nature endeared him to all with whom he came into contact. A man who seemed to have an inordinate amount of time, he managed to fill every minute of it, and much of this to the benefit of his fellow men. Noted for his ability for conciliation, his innate geniality and capacity for taking a deep and active interest in social welfare and efficient government were soon recognised, both in Torquay and, later, in Kingskerswell.

Born in 1852, he spent most of his life away from his native Uton, Crediton, coming to St Marychurch, where he was one of the first members of the St Marychurch Local Board. He met Miss Dinah Margaretta Shapley, a competent musician from Rocombe, and in 1884 they married. Mr Mortimer became hon. treasurer of the Torquay Musical Association, was one of the first members of Torquay Town Council when it became a borough in the 1890s, and was at one time Deputy Mayor to Mr William F. Ball. Later the Mortimers came to live in Kingskerswell, where their kindly influence was felt and appreciated for the remainder of their lives.

In Kingskerswell William bought Rendell's Brewery in Chestnuts in Fore Street from which he supplied about eight public houses in the district,

Chestnut House, Fore Street – one-time Tree Farm, Mr Mortimer's Brewery and, later, Stentiford's Farm. It has since been demolished and replaced by Marguerite Way. The fine chestnut tree has also gone.

including the Park Inn, and at one time also the Halfway House Inn. Chestnut House quickly became the centre of activity for the many interests of the Mortimers in the village.

Already representing Torre on the Newton Board of Guardians, William changed to represent Kingskerswell when a vacancy occurred, which post he retained until it was superseded by the New Guardian's Committee of which he was chairman of the board for most of the remainder of his life.

He was especially interested in the welfare of both children and working men. A rural district councillor from 1916, Mr Mortimer was chairman both of Kingskerswell Parish Council and the Parochial Committee.

In addition to a life full of civic and parochial service, Mr Mortimer maintained a keen interest in local sport, and was vice-president of Kingskerswell Cricket Club. On the occasion of the club's move to the then new pitch at Aller, he it was who formally opened the new cricket pavilion.

He was chairman of the Nursing Association and during the First World War was chairman of the Newton Rural District Food Control Committee, as well as being a member of the Royal Military Tribunal. Mr Mortimer, 'Billy' to his friends, was chairman and MD of the Torquay Theatre Royal in which he maintained an avid interest, until it became a cinema in the early 1930s.

His wife, Dinah Margaretta, had played the organ at Upton Church at the age of 12 and she won the Lady Goldschmidt scholarship and was an outstanding pupil at the Royal Academy of Music, gaining the coveted gold medal for pianoforte playing. Her musical talents were such that she was made an Associate of the Royal Academy. Mrs Mortimer was a founder member of the Torquay Musical Association and was instrumental in forming the Kingskerswell Choral Society and the local Mothers' Union. Of their family of nine children, Reginald lost his life in the First World War and

PERSONALITIES: A MISCELLANY

is commemorated on the War Memorial in the village, and Aubrey died young aged 32 leaving a wife and two children. The seven remaining children distinguished themselves in a manner befitting their parents. Mrs Mortimer died in December 1932, joined in eternity 21 months later by her husband.

AROUND THE WORLD IF NEED BE & ROUND THE WORLD AGAIN
(From an old sea song)

At Auckland, New Zealand, about as far as one can get from the parish of Kingskerswell, Devon, is a three-ton boulder upon which is fixed a bronze plaque. The end part of the inscription on the plaque reads, 'Dedicated by the Duder Family to mark the anniversary of the arrival in New Zealand of Thomas Duder of Kingskerswell, Devon.' Thomas Duder, born in the parish in 1806, was baptised in the then chapel of ease, St Mary the Virgin. At that time the village and its manorial lands were still part of the parish of St Mary Church. The perpetual curate of St Mary's, the Revd Aaron Neck, later to become vicar of the newly created parish of Kingskerswell, was related to the Duder family by the marriage of his daughter Agnes to Samuel, uncle of Thomas.

A New Zealander, Mrs Marianne Philson, has made great progress in tracing back her ancestry. Thanks to her perseverance, her Duder family origins can be followed without break back to John, who died in 1580 in Tiverton, Devon. John Duder's great-great-great-grandson, Humphrey, of Kingskerswell, married Ann Jago on 2 January 1763 in the Parish Church of St Mary the Virgin. Humphrey and Ann had 12 children of whom Samuel, son-in-law of the Revd Aaron Neck, was the seventh. Samuel's second eldest brother William married Margery Barter, also of Kingskerswell. William and Margery had four children, Humphrey, William, Thomas and Elizabeth Barter. Elizabeth married William Woollacott in May 1833. (The Woollacott family were notable builders in the parish at one time.)

Kingskerswell, in common with most South Devon communities, for several centuries had many of its sons involved either in seafaring, or in related occupations, a fact which was not lost on a government in the 1620s preoccupied with wars with Spain and France. A potentially readily available source of manpower, with the recognised expertise in seafaring, and with a ready source of craftsmanship to match, was soon the subject of Navy Board surveys. The names Ball, Bartar, Bickford, Codner, Cole, Crockwell, Drew, Miller, Sampson and Wills account for 24 mariners of the 55 for Kingskerswell listed in the Duke of Buckingham's Survey of 1619. Most of these names indicate long-standing family ties with the parish.

Thomas Duder, son of William and Margery, continued in the same tradition. He became apprenticed as a carpenter and shipwright at Teignmouth and at one time was a fisherman. Later on, as Able Seaman in the Royal Navy, he found himself on his way to New Zealand on HMS *Buffalo*, via Quebec, Brazil, Tasmania and Sydney. The ship carried on board a certain Thomas Cheesman, who wrote journals which have survived. Fortunately for Thomas Duder, the ship, when anchored at Cook's Bay near Whitianga, found herself in difficulties in a hurricane-force storm, and beached in Mercury Bay, two miles away. Thomas chose to stay in the new colony and gained employment in the Harbour Department, initially as 'Coxswain of the Pinnace', and later as 'Signalman at Mount Victoria'.

Later, in 1845, he married Margaret Dunne from County Wicklow, Ireland. Thomas bought land on the north shore of the harbour and started farming. This is where the commemorative rock is to be found. The land brought fortune to the family from the development of some of it for housing and the creation of one of North Island's large stores. In the early part of the twentieth century the family were to the fore of New Zealand social life with their horse racing and sailing interests.

One of Thomas' great-grandsons was Dr Robert Frederick Moody of the RNZAF, who was a prisoner in the infamous 'Colditz Castle' POW camp. One of those 'difficult, ill-disciplined and persistent escapers', according to their captors, Dr 'Fred'

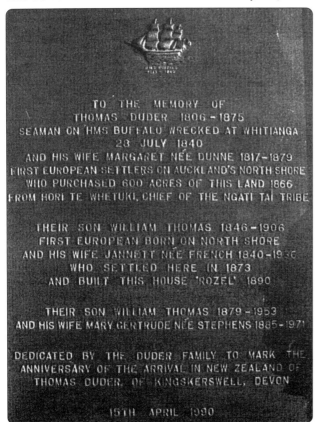

Thomas Duder memorial plaque, North Shore, Auckland, New Zealand. With acknowledgement to Marianne Philson.

certainly assisted his fellows in obtaining materials for escape schemes.

The eldest brother of Thomas was Humphrey, who married Charlotte Furneaux, and who with son William farmed at Brookador [sic], before emigrating to South Island, New Zealand. Once more the move to the colonies proved successful and prosperous.

Thomas and Humphrey's youngest Duder uncle, another Thomas, married Ann Congdon and later settled in Newfoundland. Many folk from Devon villages, including Kingskerswell, were to be found there, engaged in the fishing industry on land and water. Of their ten children the first three remained in Devon, while the fourth, John Congdon, followed later. A grandson of Thomas and Ann, Thomas Congdon Duder left the family home to live on the island of Fogo, where he started a business and in 1895 was elected to the government of Newfoundland. In 1885 a second home was built and named Devon Farm Cottage.

Thomas and Ann's sixth son, Edwin John, had an import/export business with goods exchanged for fish. He owned about 100 sailing vessels, including some locally-built schooners, aboard which he exported fish to Great Britain and Europe, Brazil and the Caribbean.

Another Newfoundland family descendant of Thomas and Ann was Dr Cluny MacPherson, who helped improve and develop the gas mask during the First World War. On his father's side Dr MacPherson is descended from Joseph Furneaux, a fish merchant of Dartmouth, Devon.

The youngest son of Samuel Duder and Agnes Neck was George, who married Frances Harvey, from Moretonhampstead on the edge of Dartmoor. In 1841 George farmed 100 acres in Kingskerswell and employed four labourers. Their second son George Harvey Duder, one of their ten children, went off to Bahia in Brazil where he started his own shipping agency. Here he met and married Constancia Wilson (her gravestone has the Portuguese orthography). Their six children were educated in England. At one time Brazil was the world's largest producer of cocoa and George Harvey Duder was the world's largest supplier of cocoa beans until the development of cocoa production in Africa.

George Harvey and Constancia lie at peace in a grave with a finely carved headstone in their home churchyard of Kingskerswell. George and Constancia's youngest son Daniel married their niece Katherine Isabel, whose brother Arthur Wrayford Duder made a partnership with a relative, a son of another Kingskerswell yeoman farmer named Barter, and founded the famous County Stores in Taunton.

Samuel, the eldest son of George and Frances, became a master mariner himself, and married Mary Ann Stooke from yet another prominent Kingskerswell family. Both Stooke and Barter families are inter-related Kingskerswell clans.

In the 1960s Campbell Leonard MacPherson had the honour of serving as Lieutenant-Governor of Newfoundland, a fitting tribute to his earliest Duder ancestor in the province. A great-great-great-grand-father of Campbell Leonard was Humphrey Duder, father-in-law of Revd Aaron Neck.

The northern foothills of the Caucasus may hold the clue to another branch of the family in the person of Yuri Duder, a Professor at Stavropol agricultural college and an old acquaintance of Mikhail Gorbachev. Yuri is George in Russian.

The Duder family maintained close ties with many other influential Kingskerswell families. The role played by seafaring has been paramount to the Duders in the advancement of their fortunes and worldwide dispersal.

Forde House, Newton Abbot, March 2001. Kingskerswell Parish Council honours retiring Parish Clerk, Mr Bert Mitchell, after 32 years' service; left to right, back row: *councillors John Newland, Norman Cooper, John Hartley, Mike Haines, Kevin Mason;* front: *councillors John Petherick, Edony Dolan, Parish Clerk Bert Mitchell, Charlotte Mertens Parish Council Chairman, Sheila Cook, Derek Miller.*

PERSONALITIES: A MISCELLANY

Left: *Induction of Mr Hollomby, the new Chairman of Kerswells Parish Council.* Left to right: Mr Buckpitt (Abbotskerswell), ?, Mr Garrick (Clerk), Mr W. Adams, Mr Bob Fraser, Mr Hollomby, ?, Mrs Honey, Mr Roly Elliott.

Right: *Dr Colin MacVicker, Chairman of Newton Abbot Rural District Council, June 1968, leaving St Mary's Church, Kingskerswell, flanked by Mrs Hilda MacVicker and the Revd Rowe.* Left to right: ?, ?, Mr Frank Banbury, ?, ?.

Left: *Mr W. Adams presents Revd A. Rowe with a cheque and bedside electric teamaker, 14 March 1970. The Revd Alan Rowe had served the parish as vicar for 39 years. He was ordained in St John's Cathedral, Newfoundland, where he married Maud in 1929.* Left to right: Mrs Maud Rowe, Mr Frank Banbury, Revd Alan F.C. Rowe, Mr J.D.M. Thomas, Mr W. Adams, Mr S. Whiteway.

Nix Family

Above: *George and Alice Nix and their son David, outside Rose Cottage, North Whilborough, 1931. The Nix family were quarry workers at Stoneycombe quarry.*

Right: *Sid and Florence Nix outside 3 Orchard Cottages, Brookador, 1943.*

Dorothy Nix outside The Hollies, North Whilborough, 1928.

Chapter 12

BARTON HALL

BARTON HALL

Sir Henry Langford, third Sheriff of Devon and a judge at Greys Inn, London, became lord of the manor of Kingskerswell in 1710. His family origins lay in Langford in Derbyshire. He left the estate to his godson, Thomas Brown, Esq., of Combsatchfield, Silverton, Devon, and Thomas passed the name Langford on to his children. Thomas Brown's great-grandson, Henry Langford Brown, built Barton Hall to a design by E.W. Gribble of Torquay in the late 1830s in the mock-Tudor style, completing it in 1840 at a cost of £10,000. The site, near the boundaries of St Marychurch and Coffinswell, was chosen because of Langford's interest in yachting. On arrival in Torquay he would fire a cannon to alert his coachman to come and meet him at the harbour.

In 1862 Barton Hall suffered a terrible event. At around 11.00p.m. on 8 April some of the servants in the Hall noticed smoke and then flames issuing from the roof of the attics. The fire-engines at Newton Abbot and Torquay were sent for but by this time the blaze had a fierce hold and the furniture and contents were being carried out as quickly as possible. The fire was left to burn itself out which it did by 8.00p.m. By then the entire building had been destroyed with the exception of part of the outbuildings at the rear. Restoration of the Hall was started immediately and the family meanwhile stayed in Fluder House, some three-quarters of a mile away, while reconstruction work continued. The rebuilt house followed the original in style, two-storied with a large carriage porch and crenellated tower.

In the late-nineteenth and early-twentieth centuries, Hercules Langford Brown was a local Justice of the Peace, and was deeply involved in both district and parish affairs. This was after a 25-year commission in the Seaforth Highlanders Militia. Untypical of many landed gentry, his preference was not the social life of others, but he was more at ease with creating things with his own hands. Fond of fly fishing, he wrote a well-received book on the subject. In his contacts with the parish he was very generous, supporting many of the Revd Fagan's improvement projects for the village. Hercules and his young artistic wife Dorothy adopted Theodora, a two-year-old orphan, whom they took to their hearts as their own. 'Theo' enjoyed as much as her adoptive parents the family's Dartmoor holidays in the mahogany horse-drawn caravan, built to a design by Hercules by the Jury firm of coachbuilders and wheelwrights in the village.

As Hercules had no direct heir to inherit the estate, the Hall passed in 1936 to Thomas Hercules Langford Brown. He did not have the chance to enjoy the property for long, however, as it was requisitioned during the Second World War by the Fire Service and the Civil Defence. On its return into his hands after the war, the Hall was in bad repair, and the grounds neglected, so Thomas was forced to sell them. They were bought by a group of Torquay businessmen, among them a Mr Liddell, and turned into a holiday complex. On 5 November 1957, Fred Pontin and his sister Elsie Brown purchased Barton Hall, Thomas retaining the rest of the estate. In 1990, Scottish and Newcastle Breweries bought Pontins and became the owners, remaining as such until 2001 when 3D Education and Adventure took over.

Barton Hall, with a kennel in the porte-cochère, c.1935.

Most large country houses are said to be haunted and Barton Hall is no exception. The Barton 'White Ghost' is said to inhabit the woods around the Hall and is reputedly the spirit of a woman murdered by her husband. Other people claim to have seen the ghost at various times but not since the early 1980s.

Barton Hall, the view from the gardens, c.1920.

Below: *Barton Hall, library, c.1920.*

A bedroom at Barton Hall, c.1920.

BARTON HALL

Barton Hall dining-room, c.1920

Left: *The Langford Brown family in the garden of Barton Hall, c.1895. Left to right, standing:* Grandfather Hercules Edwin, Beatrice Grace (Bea), Harold (father of present Squire), Hercules Langford, Edith Clementina (Clem); *seated:* Marion (Molly), Dorothy Ayre (Dolly), George Langford, grandmother Edith Clementina, Susanna (Susie).

A painting of the Langford Brown family, c.1854. Left to right, back row: Mary (great-grandmother), Mary Bridget, Hercules Edwin, Henry; *front:* Elizabeth Francis, Augustus Langford (Gussie), Sealy Langford, Emily Susan.

155

Above: *Hercules Langford Brown, Seaforth Highlanders Militia.*

Watcombe pottery jardiniere and stand, both decorated with a painting of Barton Hall.

Above: *The old smugglers tree, long known to many as the 'Bottle Tree' from a certain clandestine usage in days gone by.*

Below: *Squire Henry Langford Brown's portable 'Cab Hailer'?*

Subscribers

Lesley Ahearne, Kingskerswell, Devon

Alison and Brian Ainsworth, Kingskerswell, Devon

Mrs E.J. Allen, Bexley

John and Marjorie Anstis, Kingskerswell

Ron and Clare Baker, Kingskerswell, Devon

Martin Barber-Lafon

June, Brenda and Pam (deceased) Barnes, Kingskerswell

Julie Best (Duder Family), New Zealand

The Billington Family, Kingskerswell, Devon

Binmore, Garrett, Kingskerswell, Caldicott

Betty Birley, Kingskerswell, Devon

Stan S. Blackmore, Kingskerswell, Devon

Jennifer A. Blagdon, Kingskerswell, Devon

Mrs J. Blight, New Ash Green, Kent

J.A. Bond, Sydney, Australia

L.P. Bond, Auckland, New Zealand

Valerie Bovey (née Wyatt), Torquay, Devon

Doreen Bradford (née Moon), Kingskerswell

Dennis Bramble, Kingskerswell

Winnie and Eddie Braund, 'Simmond Lea', Kingskerswell

Doris E. Bray

Alison Brewster (née Jury), Ringwood, Hampshire

David C. Brooking, Kingskerswell

Keith Brooking, Kingskerswell

Leslie P. Brooking, Kingskerswell

Ray Brooking, Kingskerswell

Mrs V.A. Brookland

Thomas H.L. Brown, Squire of Kingskerswell

Sarah and Geoff Buck, Coffinswell, Devon

Esme Burnell, Kingskerswell

K.J. Burrow, Bucks Cross, Devon

Norman and Lucy Cann, Kingskerswell

Mr Roger F. Carnell, Ipplepen, Devon

Rebecca Carter (née Jury), Kingsteignton, Devon

Carter and Co. Insurance, Kingskerswell

Les Cheesman

Una Churchward (née Wilkinson), Daccombe

Beryl Clarke (née Jury), Runwell, Essex

Vivian Clewes, Shropshire

Michael Clifford

Norman Cole, Kingskerswell, Devon

Sue and Dave Cole, Kingskerswell

Carol Colledge, Kingskerswell, Devon

Cllr David Corney and Mr Tom Walker, Kingskerswell

Johanna Courtney

Crystal Cox (née Mugridge), Cullen, Scotland

Russell B. Crocker, Havant, Hampshire

John M. Crump, Kingskerswell, Devon

Mrs Margaret Cullis-Dixon (née German), Torquay, Devon

Peter J. Dainton, Kingskerswell, Devon

Adam and Sam Daly, Kingskerswell, Devon

Mr M.J. Daniel, Kingskerswell, Devon

Dr Stephen Dart, Kingskerswell, Devon

Fred Dodd

Rita Driver (née Nelson), Kingskerswell

Mrs E. Dunton, Abbotskerswell

Doreen J. Early, resident since 1957

Dr Brian East, Kingskerswell, Devon

Mr and Mrs R.C. Edwards, Cannington, Somerset

Michael J. Egerton, Ipplepen, Devon

Mrs Anna E. Eggleton, Kingskerswell, Devon

The Elliott Family, Kingskerswell

Bruce Embury, Newton Abbot

Col Max Embury O.B.E. DL, Broadhempston

Sharon Embury, Kingskerswell

Roger England, Kingskerswell

Violet Evans, Kingskerswell, Devon

Albert and Dorothy (née Hurrell) Evemy, Huxnor Road, Kingskerswell

Christopher and Linda Evemy, Huxnor Road, Kingskerswell/now Essex

Ms Annette Everett, Kingskerswell, Devon

Vanessa Everton
R. and J. Facey (née Webber), Torquay, Devon
Dorothy Fogwill, Kingskerswell
Daphne and Veronica Foot, Kingskerswell, Devon
Arthur French, Ipplepen, Devon
Pat Furneaux, Kingskerswell, Devon
B. Gale, Shrewton, Salisbury, Wiltshire
R. Gale, Kingskerswell, Devon
Sydney Gale, Kingskerswell, Devon. 1916–2003
Mrs Joy Garner (née Howard), Newton Abbot
Paul R. Gerry, Kingskerswell, Devon
Muriel Ann Gigg, Kingskerswell
S.A. Glendinning, Kingskerswell, Devon
Maureen Gooch
Les Grant, Kingskerswell
Mrs Barbara and Mr Les Haines, Kingskerswell 1971–98
Ivan C. Harding (deceased), late of St Mary's Garage, Kingskerswell
Noel Harvey-Webb, Te Aroha, N.Z.
John Hawkins, Kingskerswell
Barry E. Hayman, Kingskerswell
Rosemary E. Haywood, Kingskerswell, Devon
Mrs Alice Herbert, Kingskerswell, Devon
Mr Maurice S. Herbert, Shiphay, Torquay, Devon
Bernard C. Hill, Kingskerswell, Devon
Jean Hill, Exeter, Devon
Roy S. Hill, Kingskerswell, Devon
The Hill Family, The Old Bakery, Kingskerswell
David J.K. Honeywill, Newton Abbot, Devon
A. Robin Hood, Barton, Torquay
Elizabeth A.D. Hooper, Ashburton, Devon
Pamela Howard, Kingskerswell
Mrs S.E. Howitt, Kingskerswell
Janet Humphrey, Kingskerswell, Devon
Terry George Hutchings, Kingskerswell, Devon
Trevor J. Hutchings, Kingskerswell
Peter Hutton, N.S.W., Australia
Mary M.A. Jackson
Dorothy Jennings, Kingskerswell
Miss C.E. Jerman, Princess Road, Kingskerswell, Devon
Mr D. Johns, Kingskerswell, Devon
Alfred W.E. Jury, Swainswick, Bath
Margaret Jury, Kingskerswell, Devon

Robert Edmond Jury
Peter E. Kenyon, Kingskerswell
Janet King (née Hodge-Brooks), Kingskerswell
Maggie King, Kingskerswell, Devon
Kingskerswell Twinning Association
Jacqueline and William Kirkham, Whilborough, Kingskerswell
Mr H.E. Knapman, Kingskerswell, Devon
Mrs Joan Knapman (née Brenton), Kingskerswell
Michael Knapman, formerly of 2 Carswells Estate
Mrs Jacqueline Lake, Kingskerswell, Devon
Paul Lang, Newton Abbot, Devon
Stanley and Rosalind Lavis, Newton Abbot, Devon
Pauline A. Lawrence, Kingskerswell, Devon
Doreen M. Looker, Kingskerswell, Devon
Mrs Suzanne Lovell, Kingskerswell, Devon
Graham A. and Susan E. Luscombe, Kingskerswell, Devon
Phil, Yvonne, Emma and Andrew Maker, Kingskerswell
Christine Margetts (née Pain), Elliot Lake, Canada
Janet Masters, Swindon
Caroline and Kingsley Matthews, Kingskerswell
Margaret Matthews (née Jury), Kingskerswell, Devon
M.P. McElheron, Kingskerswell
Molly and James Meakin, Kingskerswell, Devon
Charlotte L.H. Mertens
Frank Middlebrook, Kingskerswell, Devon
Bert Mitchell, Kingskerswell, Devon
Roy J. Mitchell, Kingskerswell, Devon
Mrs Patricia A. Moon, Kingskerswell, Devon
Roger Ian Moon, Kingskerswell, Devon
Roy Moon's Family, Kingskerswell, Devon
Mr and Mrs Stephen John Moon, Kingskerswell, Devon
Harold Robert Mudge, River Edge, New Jersey, USA
Alexander and Thelma P. Murray, North Whilborough, Kingskerswell
Vic and Faye Myers, St Marys, Kingskerswell
Helen Nelder, Kingsteignton, Devon
Joan Nelson (née Mills), Kingskerswell

SUBSCRIBERS

Joan and Dennis Noble, Kingskerswell
Robert Norman, Kingskerswell, Devon
Steve and Kay Oram, Kingskerswell, Devon
Derek and Barbara Orton, Kingskerswell, Devon
Tony Pain, Coles Lane, Kingskerswell
Gwen and Gerry Palmer, Kingskerswell
Mr R. Peters, Newton Abbot, Devon
John Lionel Petherick, Kingskerswell, Devon
Neil Phillips, Auckland, New Zealand
Marianne Philson (née Duder), Auckland, New Zealand
Jayne Pritchard, Kingskerswell, Devon
Gordon Quant, Lane Park, N. Wilborough, Kingskerswell
Gerald F. Quinn, Torquay, Devon
Sheila and Jim Read, Kingskerswell
Lisa J. Ridley (née Bovey), Oakwood, Derbyshire
Ethel Phyllis Roberts, Widow
Gill Roberts, Brookedor, Kingskerswell, Devon
Ian Roberts, High Wycombe, Buckinghamshire
Kelvin H. Roberts, Yeovil, Somerset
Mr and Mrs P. Roberts
Mr W. Edgar Roberts, Kingskerswell, Devon
Deborah Rollins, Exeter, Devon
Vi Rowe, Kingskerswell, Devon
Alan Salsbury, Stoneycombe, Devon
Sheila Sercombe (née Pain), Preston, Paignton
The Sharam Family, Kingskerswell
Wendy J. Shillabeer, Kingskerswell, Devon
Frank and Jean Shine, Kingskerswell, Devon
Matthew J. Short, Kingskerswell
M.A.R. Skedgell, Kingskerswell, Devon
Elaine Smerdon (née Gale), Kingskerswell
Betty G. Smith (née Fogwill), Haroldhill, Essex
Margare J. Smith, Kingskerswell
The Spencer Family, Kingskerswell
Jan Stainer (née Edwards), Kingskerswell
Nicholas M. Stentiford
Timothy R. Stentiford

Mrs Rena Stephenson (née Brown), Kingskerswell
Mrs Olive Stevens (née Roberts)
Philip and Mo Stevens, Kingskerswell
Jim Stidworthy, Oldham, Lancashire
John A. Stolworthy, Kingskerswell, Devon
Stella M. Stone, Kingskerswell, Devon
Sue and Mike Sutton, Kingskerswell, Devon
Jack Swann, Torquay, Devon
Mrs Olive N. Thomas, Southey Lane, Kingskerswell
Bryan D. Titcomb, formerly of Yon Street, Kingskerswell, Devon
E.S. Trewin (née Stentiford), Chestnut House, Kingskerswell
Diane, Glenn and Joshua Trigwell, Kingskerswell
Sean M. Tucker, Torquay, Devon
Laura M. Underhill, Kingskerswell
Philip R. Underhill, Kingskerswell
William G. Underhill, Kingskerswell, Devon
Miss A.R. Wakeham, Kingskerswell
Mrs B.B. Jane Wale
Mr W.H. Hicks Wale, Southport
Richard Wale, Kings Heath, Birmingham
The Walker Family
John F.W. Walling, Newton Abbot, Devon
Mr and Mrs John Watts, Kingskerswell, Devon
Mr and Mrs R.J. Weatherley
Joy Welch (née Hutton), Torquay, Devon
Patrick J. White, Kingskerswell, Devon
David, Janet, Stephen and Anne Whittaker
Lynda Wills, Kingskerswell, Devon
Philip H.J. Wills, Torquay, Devon
Gillian Wright (granddaughter of W.M. Jury), Kingskerswell, Devon
David Wyatt, Exeter, Devon
Eileen Rosemary Wyatt, Abbotskerswell, Devon
Robert John Wyatt, Kingskerswell, Devon
Paul J. Wylie, Kingskerswell, Devon
Roger B. Wyse, Kingskerswell, Devon

THE BOOK OF KINGSKERSWELL

Community Histories

The Book of Addiscombe • Canning and Clyde Road Residents Association and Friends
The Book of Addiscombe, Vol. II • Canning and Clyde Road Residents Association and Friends
The Book of Axminster with Kilmington • L. Berry and G. Gosling
The Book of Bampton • Caroline Seward
The Book of Barnstaple • Avril Stone
The Book of Barnstaple, Vol. II • Avril Stone
The Book of The Bedwyns • Bedwyn History Society
The Book of Bickington • Stuart Hands
Blandford Forum: A Millennium Portrait • Blandford Forum Town Council
The Book of Bramford • Bramford Local History Group
The Book of Breage & Germoe • Stephen Polglase
The Book of Bridestowe • D. Richard Cann
The Book of Bridport • Rodney Legg
The Book of Brixham • Frank Pearce
The Book of Buckfastleigh • Sandra Coleman
The Book of Buckland Monachorum & Yelverton • Pauline Hamilton-Leggett
The Book of Carharrack • Carharrack Old Cornwall Society
The Book of Carshalton • Stella Wilks and Gordon Rookledge
The Parish Book of Cerne Abbas • Vivian and Patricia Vale
The Book of Chagford • Iain Rice
The Book of Chapel-en-le-Frith • Mike Smith
The Book of Chittlehamholt with Warkleigh & Satterleigh • Richard Lethbridge
The Book of Chittlehampton • Various
The Book of Colney Heath • Bryan Lilley
The Book of Constantine • Moore and Trethowan
The Book of Cornwood & Lutton • Compiled by the People of the Parish
The Book of Creech St Michael • June Small
The Book of Cullompton • Compiled by the People of the Parish
The Book of Dawlish • Frank Pearce
The Book of Dulverton, Brushford, Bury & Exebridge • Dulverton and District Civic Society
The Book of Dunster • Hilary Binding
The Book of Edale • Gordon Miller
The Ellacombe Book • Sydney R. Langmead
The Book of Exmouth • W.H. Pascoe
The Book of Grampound with Creed • Bane and Oliver
The Book of Hayling Island & Langstone • Peter Rogers
The Book of Helston • Jenkin with Carter
The Book of Hemyock • Clist and Dracott
The Book of Herne Hill • Patricia Jenkyns
The Book of Hethersett • Hethersett Society Research Group
The Book of High Bickington • Avril Stone
The Book of Ilsington • Dick Wills
The Book of Kingskerswell • Carsewella Local History Group
The Book of Lamerton • Ann Cole and Friends
Lanner, A Cornish Mining Parish • Sharron Schwartz and Roger Parker
The Book of Leigh & Bransford • Malcolm Scott
The Book of Litcham with Lexham & Mileham • Litcham Historical and Amenity Society
The Book of Loddiswell • Loddiswell Parish History Group
The New Book of Lostwithiel • Barbara Fraser
The Book of Lulworth • Rodney Legg
The Book of Lustleigh • Joe Crowdy
The Book of Lyme Regis • Rodney Legg
The Book of Manaton • Compiled by the People of the Parish

The Book of Markyate • Markyate Local History Society
The Book of Mawnan • Mawnan Local History Group
The Book of Meavy • Pauline Hemery
The Book of Minehead with Alcombe • Binding and Stevens
The Book of Morchard Bishop • Jeff Kingaby
The Book of Newdigate • John Callcut
The Book of Nidderdale • Nidderdale Museum Society
The Book of Northlew with Ashbury • Northlew History Group
The Book of North Newton • J.C. and K.C. Robins
The Book of North Tawton • Baker, Hoare and Shields
The Book of Nynehead • Nynehead & District History Society
The Book of Okehampton • R. and U. Radford
The Book of Paignton • Frank Pearce
The Book of Penge, Anerley & Crystal Palace • Peter Abbott
The Book of Peter Tavy with Cudlipptown • Peter Tavy Heritage Group
The Book of Pimperne • Jean Coull
The Book of Plymtree • Tony Eames
The Book of Porlock • Dennis Corner
Postbridge – The Heart of Dartmoor • Reg Bellamy
The Book of Priddy • Albert Thompson
The Book of Princetown • Dr Gardner-Thorpe
The Book of Rattery • By the People of the Parish
The Book of St Day • Joseph Mills and Paul Annear
The Book of Sampford Courtenay with Honeychurch • Stephanie Pouya
The Book of Sculthorpe • Gary Windeler
The Book of Seaton • Ted Gosling
The Book of Sidmouth • Ted Gosling and Sheila Luxton
The Book of Silverton • Silverton Local History Society
The Book of South Molton • Jonathan Edmunds
The Book of South Stoke with Midford • Edited by Robert Parfitt
South Tawton & South Zeal with Sticklepath • R. and U. Radford
The Book of Sparkwell with Hemerdon & Lee Mill • Pam James
The Book of Staverton • Pete Lavis
The Book of Stithians • Stithians Parish History Group
The Book of Stogumber, Monksilver, Nettlecombe & Elworthy • Maurice and Joyce Chidgey
The Book of Studland • Rodney Legg
The Book of Swanage • Rodney Legg
The Book of Tavistock • Gerry Woodcock
The Book of Thorley • Sylvia McDonald and Bill Hardy
The Book of Torbay • Frank Pearce
The Book of Watchet • Compiled by David Banks
The Book of West Huntspill • By the People of the Parish
Widecombe-in-the-Moor • Stephen Woods
Widecombe – Uncle Tom Cobley & All • Stephen Woods
The Book of Williton • Michael Williams
The Book of Witheridge • Peter and Freda Tout and John Usmar
The Book of Withycombe • Chris Boyles
Woodbury: The Twentieth Century Revisited • Roger Stokes
The Book of Woolmer Green • Compiled by the People of the Parish

For details of any of the above titles or if you are interested in writing your own history, please contact: Commissioning Editor Community Histories, Halsgrove House, Lower Moor Way, Tiverton Business Park, Tiverton, Devon EX16 6SS, England; email: naomic@halsgrove.com

In order to include as many historical photographs as possible in this volume, a printed index is not included. However, the Devon titles in the Community History Series are indexed by Genuki. For further information and indexes to various volumes in the series, please visit: http://www.cs.ncl.ac.uk/genuki/DEV/indexingproject.html